The Power of Neuroplasticity for Pastoral and Spiritual Care

The Power of Neuroplasticity for Pastoral and Spiritual Care

Kirk A. Bingaman

LEXINGTON BOOKS
Lanham • Boulder • New York • Toronto • Plymouth, UK

Published by Lexington Books
A wholly owned subsidiary of Rowman & Littlefield
4501 Forbes Boulevard, Suite 200, Lanham, Maryland 20706
www.rowman.com

10 Thornbury Road, Plymouth PL6 7PP, United Kingdom

British Library Cataloguing in Publication Information Available

Library of Congress Cataloging-in-Publication Data

Bingaman, Kirk A.
The power of neuroplasticity for pastoral and spiritual care / Kirk Bingaman. pages cm
Includes bibliographical references.
ISBN 978-0-7391-7538-5 (cloth : alk. paper)— 978-0-7391-7539-2 (electronic)
1. Neuroplasticity. 2. Pastoral counseling. I. Title.
QP360.5B55 2014
612.8—dc23
2014008770
ISBN 978-0-7391-9397-6 (pbk : alk. paper)

Printed in the United States of America

Contents

Acknowledgments

I am grateful for the generous support and guidance I have received from so many people and colleagues. One does not create a project like this in a vacuum, charting a new path of research into a variety of different fields and disciplines. I thank the staff of Lexington Books: my editor, Eric Wrona, for his enthusiastic support and careful attention with multiple drafts of the manuscript; my assistant editor, Emily Frazzette, for her helpful and collaborative approach readying the manuscript for production; and assistant managing editor, Della Vache, for her guidance with the production process and unexpected suggestion for the title of the book. Fordham University and its Office of Research awarded me a faculty fellowship and sabbatical to work on the project, which provided a valuable opportunity to give it my undivided attention and focus. I am grateful to the dean of the Graduate School of Religion and Religious Education, Dr. C. Colt Anderson, for his support of the fellowship and project, along with my pastoral care and counseling colleagues, Drs. Lisa Cataldo and Mary Beth Werdel. Fr. John Cecero, S.J. and Drs. Bradford Hinze and Warren Tryon, of Fordham University, reviewed and commented on an early proposal of the project, supplying me with generous and useful feedback.

The project began taking shape over the course of several years, primarily in the context of the Group for New Directions in Pastoral Theology. I thank Drs. Robert Dykstra and Donald Capps of Princeton Theological Seminary, and my other colleagues in the group, for supporting my early research into neuroscience and pastoral care and counseling and for the timely feedback about methodology. Additionally, I am grateful to the journal, *Pastoral Psychology*, and its editor, Dr. Lewis Rambo, and publisher, Springer, for the kind permission to publish earlier research (see References). The Psychology, Culture, and Religion Group of the American Academy of Religion has been another source of support and encouragement, with its members representing a breadth of different research interests and viewpoints. I am grateful to my colleagues at the Lutheran Counseling Center of New York, for their curiosity about my research and encouragement with the project, and to the Zen Garland community in Airmont, NY, for the sacred space to regularly engage in contemplative-meditational practice. To the First Presbyterian Church in Cold Spring, NY, where I have given workshops, retreats, and sermons on the topic, and particularly to Norman and Lynn Brown, thank you for the interest you have shown in my work. And, I thank the Rev. Dr. Douglas Huneke for the many telephone conversations and for your interest in my research as it has evolved over the years. Finally, I am grateful to Annie for your love and support and the way you live your life contemplatively and mindfully.

Introduction

The extraordinary advances in neuroscience in recent years have begun to influence the study of religion, theology, and spirituality. Indeed, the emerging field of contemplative neuroscience (Davidson, 2012, p. 196) reflects a growing interest in what neuroscientific studies reveal about what is most fundamental to religious faith and the spiritual life. In the past few years my own research has increasingly focused on important neuroscientific findings regarding the plasticity and malleability of the human brain to make the case for greater use of contemplative and meditational practices in pastoral and spiritual care. This is based on the discovery that the brain "is built for change via the process of neuroplasticity, which refers to the ability of the brain to change its structure and function" (Newberg, 2010, pp. 4–5). At the same time, a growing body of research is revealing that mindfulness and contemplative spiritual practices have the capacity to balance the brain's well documented negativity bias, thus generating less fearful and anxious perspectives on life and human relationships. Consequently, I will be arguing for the elevation of such spiritual practices (e.g., mindfulness meditation, the contemplative practice of the Centering Prayer, the *Spiritual Exercises* of St. Ignatius, etc.) to a level of comparable importance with religious belief and doctrine so that pastoral and spiritual care providers are better equipped to help foster health and wellness with congregants and clients. Through the application of neuroscientific research to pastoral and clinical practice, it is possible to begin putting forward a contextual model of pastoral care and counseling that represents a necessary paradigm shift for the age of neuroscience.

Studies have revealed that a focus on mindfulness meditation and contemplative spiritual practice has the capacity to increase our non-anxious awareness and therefore significantly lower our stress more so than a focus

1

on "right belief" or correct doctrine. As such, not only do these findings have important implications for pastoral counselors and psychotherapists, they perhaps will even necessitate a paradigmatic shift in the way that clergy approach the general pastoral care of souls. A contemplative-neuroscientific approach to pastoral care and counseling is in accord, methodologically, with the correlational framework put forward by Paul Tillich, where the resources of the Judeo-Christian faith tradition are intentionally juxtaposed and even held in dialectical tension with other fields and disciplines that investigate the present cultural milieu. For example, Jesus' teaching from the Sermon on the Mount, which encourages us not to be anxious about tomorrow (Matthew 6:34), takes on a deeper practical relevance when aligned, correlationally, with compelling neuroscientific research on the plasticity and malleability of the brain. In so doing, practitioners can begin to develop a more precise method of pastoral and spiritual care that intentionally seeks, in the words of Rebecca Chopp, commenting on feminist theory and theology, "a correlation between the contemporary situation and the core of Christianity" (1997, p. 217). According to Tillich, pastoral theology and pastoral practice "must use the immense and profound material of the existential analysis in all cultural realms, including therapeutic psychology," so that it is adequate both to the Christian message "and to the human predicament as rediscovered in contemporary culture" (1999, pp. 108–109). For Tillich, of course, "the cognitive neurosciences were not yet available for incorporation into his analysis of the interrelationship between the sources of theology and the experience of religion," and yet we can reasonably infer that if living today he would focus on a similar correlation of neuroscientific research and spiritual practice as "capable of providing not only a subjective assessment of religious experience, but a biological one as well" (Newberg, 2010, p. 12).

Building on Tillich's correlational method of theological reflection and pastoral practice, and moving it a step further, David Tracy focuses on developing a criteria of "relative adequacy" to the contemporary situation in order "to assess the coherence or incoherence of any possibility with what we otherwise know or, more likely, believe to be the case" (1994, p. 91). What we know or believe to be the case from Scripture and correlationally from medical research and clinical practice is that stress and anxiety are not conducive to our overall health and well-being, that it is very much in our long-term best interests to find ways not to be anxious about tomorrow. But because of the brain's built-in bias or predisposition toward anxious rather than non-anxious awareness, this will at times be easier said than done. By acknowledging and integrating this "negativity bias" into a consideration of pastoral and clinical practice, we are better able to help anxious clients and congregants develop the capacity to monitor and modulate internal states of fear and distress. Thus, a basic understanding of the brain's hardwiring and, more specifically, its deeply ingrained negativity bias, becomes the starting point for developing a therapeutic approach that can help those in our care learn to observe and regulate their anxious thoughts and feelings. In the context of mindfulness- and acceptance-based approaches to counseling and therapy, for example, which build on the findings of neuroscientific research, the use of meditational practice is central to the therapeutic work because it helps the individual develop a mindful and transcendent awareness of his or her own internal experiences. As we will see in later chapters, this allows anxious individuals to "disentangle from ideas of themselves that have developed over their lifetimes, such as 'I am a nervous wreck'" (Roemer & Orsillo, 2009, p. 132).

A contemplative-neuroscientific approach to pastoral and spiritual care again represents something of a paradigm shift in the care of souls, for it recognizes the growing body of research that reveals "activities involving meditation and intensive prayer permanently strengthen neural functioning in specific parts of the brain that are involved with lowering anxiety and depression, enhancing social awareness and empathy, and improving cognitive and intellectual functioning" (Newberg, 2009, p. 149). This correlational and complementary investigation would no doubt be of interest to Tillich, for it provides new and important data from another "cultural realm": the importance and necessity of elevating contemplative-meditational practice to comparable standing with religious belief-doctrine. As neuroscience begins to impact and inform the field of pastoral care and counseling, it will be necessary to invite and encourage those in our care to develop a daily contemplative-meditational practice even as we help them reflect on the significance of their religious and spiritual beliefs. This will at times seem counterintuitive in the context of Western Christianity, which historically and even presently has focused more on right belief and correct doctrine than on contemplative spirituality. Throughout the centuries, the latter has often been considered the primary domain of the Desert Fathers and Mothers, the Christian mystics, and those engaged in monastic life and religious orders. By contrast, the average Christian congregant worshiping in the pews is encouraged to reflect on the essential tenets of the Christian faith, to recite the creeds, and to engage in the collective liturgical rituals of Christian worship often without a similar emphasis on developing a daily spiritual practice. Nor do seminaries, by and large, make contemplative practice a curricular priority for students aspiring to be ministers and pastoral care providers, even in an age when stress and anxiety are on the rise. The paradigmatic turn toward an awareness of the reality of neuroplasticity and the practical implications for pastoral and spiritual care will necessitate a reordering of pastoral and clinical priorities, as we begin to recognize that through a daily practice of contemplative prayer and meditation the average congregant or client can over time rewire the neural pathways of his or her brain for the better. By learning to calm the fear and stress regions of the brain, we are able to experience more tangibly and fully the peace and joy of God's presence.

The revolutionary discovery concerning neuroplasticity provides both challenges and opportunities for pastoral care and counseling because of the field's uniquely correlative position at the crossroads of theology and contemporary culture. But while there is a growing interest in the correlation and complementarity of neuroscience and religion and theology, there are few resources that give clear guidance to pastoral and spiritual care providers in terms of how to begin incorporating the findings from neuroscientific research into their work with anxious clients and congregants. As we have learned from medical science, it is particularly advantageous to our long-term mental and physical health, not to mention our spiritual well-being, to find ways to be, in the words of Jesus, less anxious about tomorrow. And, while most of us have an intellectual grasp of Jesus' teaching, heretofore we have been less clear and perhaps even less certain about its practical application to everyday life. The twin discoveries of neuroplasticity *and* the fact that it can to some extent be self-directed through various practices of mindfulness meditation and contemplative prayer now gives clearer insight and direction to pastoral practitioners looking to make more informed and effective interventions with the anxious in their care. This is not to suggest that a focus on religious beliefs and doctrines is unimportant and/or that contemplative-meditational practice is meant to supersede the creeds and theological teachings of the church. Longitudinal studies focusing on the daily practice of contemplative prayer and meditation, as we will see, demonstrate that while the benefits of prayer and meditation have much to do with the development of contemplative techniques of mindful breathing, relaxation, and, in the tradition of Centering Prayer, a focused attention upon a religious or spiritual concept that evokes comfort and peace, the more we can clarify and understand our beliefs about the focus of our meditation or prayer the more meaningful the experience will be.

The findings from neuroscientific studies have interesting parallels with the purpose of prayer and meditation for certain contemplative practitioners, such as Thomas Merton. For Merton, meditational and prayerful practices have less to do with reasoning about the essential dogmas of faith and the creeds of the church than with grounding us in "the simple presence of God" and "in direct and simple attention to reality" (1971, p. 45). Meditational practice, from the standpoint of contemplative neuroscience, is also a matter of harnessing our attention and deepening our awareness in order to quiet the chatter of the mind caused by an excessive amount of activity in the limbic region of the brain. "We are now discovering," writes the noted researcher Daniel Siegel, "how the careful focus of attention amplifies neuroplasticity by stimulating the release of neurochemicals that enhance the structural growth of synaptic linkages among the activated neurons" (2011, p. 42). The careful and intentional focus of attention, in other words, encourages neuro-plasticity by stimulating the firing of specific neurochemicals that enhance personal growth and well-being while simultaneously quieting areas of the brain associated with stress and anxiety. As we are learning, this careful focusing of attention occurs quintessentially in the context of mindfulness meditation and contemplative prayer, where new and more healthful synaptic linkages and neural pathways are created. Similarly, the mindful focus of attention and awareness is at the heart of contemplative prayer and medita-tion, which in the words of Merton "is not confined to religious reflections" but rather "implies serious mental activity and a certain absorption or con-centration which does not permit our faculties to wander off at random or to remain slack and undirected" (1960, p. 52).

Unbeknownst to Merton when he wrote this was the fact that the contem-plative approach he was putting forward would have a striking resonance with neuroscientific research, particularly the discovery that the brain is built for change through the fostering of mindful awareness and concentration. In coming chapters we will explore in greater detail the potential that daily contemplative-meditational practice offers for using the mind to change the brain. As we learn to center and ground ourselves in a mindful and contem-plative awareness of God's steadfast presence, we are better able to stimulate and amplify the neurocircuitry necessary for cultivating a grateful heart while quieting other neurocircuitry that makes us feel anxious about tomorrow. In defining the nature and purpose of contemplative spiritual practice, Merton seems to be hinting at a similar careful and mindful focus of attention:

> Contemplation is the highest expression of [human] intellectual and spiritual life. It is that life itself, fully awake, fully active, fully aware that it is alive. It is spiritual wonder. It is spontaneous awe at the sacredness of life, of being. It is gratitude, for awareness and for being. It is a vivid realization of the fact that life and being in us proceed from an invisible, transcendent, and infinitely abundant Source. Contemplation is, above all, awareness of the reality of that Source (2007, p. 1).

Building on the correlational method of pastoral theology and practice, I will be exploring in greater detail in the coming chapters the contemporary situa-tion of neuroscientific research and how this offers a clearer and more nu-anced understanding of *how* we can put into practice the core teaching of Jesus from the Sermon on the Mount: Do not be anxious about tomorrow. While pastoral and spiritual caregivers generally have a clear understanding of the substance and meaning of Jesus' words, there is often less clarity about *how* to help those in our care, and perhaps even ourselves, put this central teaching into everyday practice. Toward this end, we will begin in chapter one with the revolutionary discovery that the human brain, far from being fixed and unchanging after the early stages of human development, is instead built for change and rewiring across the entire lifespan. The reality of neuro-plasticity, that the brain is more malleable than was once thought and that its functioning *and* structural connections can be changed, holds great promise for pastoral and spiritual caregivers working with anxious clients and congre-gants. We are learning more about how we can use the mind to change the brain, or more specifically how mindfulness practices of meditation and con-templative prayer can create new and alter existing neural structures. Siegel notes from his research that "if we can awaken our minds to move our brains in a certain direction of growth, we can...use the mind to transform our brains and our lives" (2010, p. 7). While this is indeed good news for pastoral and clinical practitioners, it will come with a qualifier in chapter two that serves as something of a reality check: using the mind to change the brain holds great promise as long as we remember that the brain comes with a built-in negativity bias and predisposition toward anxious and vigilant aware-ness. As we try to put into practice the central teaching of Jesus, to center ourselves in the gift of today and to worry less about tomorrow, we will discover that the anxious brain makes this far easier said than done. Follow-ing this fundamental spiritual teaching will therefore run counter to neural undercurrents that are deeply ingrained in the human brain and central ner-vous system. It is important for pastoral and spiritual practitioners to be sure that they are not reinforcing this negativity bias, despite the very best of professional and theological intentions. For example, in chapter three we will focus on Judeo-Christian theology, specifically the theology of original sin in order for pastoral and spiritual caregivers to see that applying it injudiciously and indiscriminately in pastoral and clinical practice may have the unin-tended consequence of reinforcing the individual's anxious awareness and pessimism about herself, her life, and her relationships. If we view ourselves and those in our care as originally sinful and guilty, from the standpoint of neuroscience this has the potential to stoke the firing of neurons in the brain that keep us consistently on alert and on edge. Thus, if we are not careful, the path toward neuroplasticity and calming the anxious brain can be obstructed or blocked at times by certain views that, while perhaps being "theologically sound," stand in need of immediate reassessment based on what we are learning from neuroscience. I will therefore be offering a paradigmatic revi-sioning of the Adamic myth of original sin, which reflects the view that the great psychological and spiritual challenge of the present day and age is coming to terms with our personal and collective anxiety.

In chapter four, we will turn our attention to contemplative-meditational practice, and explore how it has become for many neuroscientific researchers the definitive way to calm the fear and stress regions of the brain. The spiritual value of prayer and meditation has long been recognized by pastoral and spiritual caregivers, but up until now there has been less understanding of the psychophysiological benefits of maintaining a daily spiritual practice.

Thus, the tendency does exist to focus more on the content of contemplative spiritual practice, *what* the individual is praying for or about rather than on the specific method of prayer and meditation or *how* he or she prays and meditates. In view of recent brain science, we will see that *how* we approach contemplative-meditational practice is not insignificant, nor is it even secondary to the spiritual content. For example, learning to manage the myriad contents of the mind that will inevitably flood our awareness while engaged in daily prayer and meditation, more specifically learning to develop a mindful and non-judgmental awareness of the wide range of our internal experiences, increases the likelihood that over time our contemplative-meditational practices will result in a reduction of stress and anxiety in the mind, brain, and body. The operative phrase to keep in mind is *over time*, lest those in our care assume that we are simply offering another quick-fix solution to the already bloated genre of self-help resources. Nor does a mindful and non-judgmental awareness of our mental contents suggest an escape from the "shadow side" of human experience, for the fundamental purpose of contemplative-meditational practice is ultimately to deepen our awareness of and engagement with the totality of life in all its fullness.

Chapter five will highlight mindfulness- and acceptance-based approaches to counseling and therapy, in order to introduce pastoral and spiritual caregivers to several therapeutic modalities that intentionally engage and are informed by the findings of neuroscience. This will provide a more precise and in-depth therapeutic framework with which to situate our work and interventions with anxious clients and congregants. As those in our care learn to more carefully focus their attention and awareness in the context of mindfulness-based pastoral and spiritual care and at home with their own mindfulness-based meditational practice, they will be better able in their daily lives to more skillfully use the mind to rewire the brain. Finally, in chapter six, we will be introduced to case material from specific mindfulness- and acceptance-based therapies, which will highlight various techniques and practices that correlate positively with a reduction in stress and anxiety. Mindfulness-Based Cognitive Therapy (MBCT), for example, emphasizes the fundamental importance of daily mindfulness meditation for moving beyond an anxious and ruminating state of mind toward a mode of mind that is more relaxed and grounded in the present moment, whatever the set of circumstances, external *and* internal, happen to be at any given moment. Acceptance and Commitment Therapy (ACT), another more recent therapeutic framework informed by neuroscientific studies, also encourages clients to engage in a daily spiritual practice of meditation and prayer so that they can learn to accept rather than avoid the totality of their internal experiences. In learning "just to sit with" our anxious thoughts and feelings, to simply be mindful of them rather than feeling a compulsion to fight with them, which is really fighting with ourselves, we are calming and soothing the region of the brain that drives our anxiety and fear. My hope is that through this book pastoral and spiritual caregivers will find the means to develop a basic conceptual and practical framework for situating their work with anxious clients and congregants, one that is more precisely informed by the timely findings emerging from the world of neuroscience.

Chapter One

The Plasticity of the Human Brain

And men go forth to wonder at the heights of mountains, the huge waves of the sea, the broad flow of the rivers, the extent of the ocean, and the course of the stars, and omit to wonder at themselves. —St. Augustine, *Confessions*

Early in 2013, President Obama announced plans to begin a scientific initiative to explore the inner workings of the human brain and to build an extensive map of its activity, comparable in scope to the Human Genome Project. The project "will include federal agencies, private foundations, and teams of neuroscientists and nanoscientists in a concerted effort to advance the knowledge of the brain's billions of neurons and gain greater insights into perception, actions, and ultimately, consciousness" (Markoff, 2013, p. A1). In the coming years, we will no doubt acquire a much better and more specific understanding of the complexity of the human brain, and how its cells or neurons interact and communicate with each other. Already we know that there are more than one hundred billion neurons in the brain, and that each neuron is connected to other neurons by way of ten thousand or more synaptic connections or linkages. If we are bold enough to attempt the math, we discover that there are hundreds of trillions of synaptic connections linking the brain's neural groupings, a calculation that is something like "ten to the millionth power—or ten times ten one million times" (Siegel, 2011, p. 38). If this does not stagger the imagination enough, the vast number of synapses connecting the neurons in the brain is believed to exceed the number of atoms in the universe. Thus, "even if we wanted to, we could not live long enough to count each of those synaptic linkages," let alone "experience in one lifetime even a small percentage of these firing possibilities" (Siegel, 2011, p. 38). While we have much to learn about the inner workings and activity of the brain, we are at least beginning to grasp the importance of the "neuroplastic principle," that the repeated firing of neurons in specific areas

9

of the brain can strengthen, reinforce, and/or change the synaptic connections within and between those areas. An important practical lesson for pastoral and spiritual caregivers to glean from the neuroscientific research, one with major implications for ourselves and those in our care, is that "neuroplastic changes not only reveal structural alterations, but they are accompanied by changes in brain function, mental experience (such as feelings and emotional balance), and bodily states (such as response to stress and immune function)" (Siegel, 2007, p. 32).

HARNESSING THE POWER OF MINDFUL AWARENESS

The "power of neuroplasticity" has been articulated by such notable researchers as Richard Davidson, working in the field of affective and contemplative neuroscience that focuses on the study of the brain basis of human emotion, Andrew Newberg, a pioneer in the study of neurophysiology and its application to religious and spiritual experience, and Daniel Siegel, whose research into interpersonal neurobiology and the practice of "mindsight," the mindful awareness of the inner workings of the mind and brain, helps us to see the possibilities for cultivating wellness and neural integration in daily life. Siegel, for example, notes that "by harnessing the power of awareness to strategically stimulate the brain's firing, mindsight enables us to voluntarily change a firing pattern that was laid down involuntarily" (2011, p. 42). Far from being fixed and unchanging, the human brain has a profound capacity for change, continued growth, and transformation of its own functioning *and* structure. And, this is not merely limited to the formative years of childhood and adolescence or even early adulthood for that matter, as certain developmental theories have previously suggested. Rather, the potential for neuroplasticity that is abundantly evident at the beginning of life extends across the human life cycle, and therefore is also available until the end of life. Put another way, "neuroplasticity is not just available to us in youth: we now know that it can occur throughout the lifespan" (2011, p. 5). The creation of wholly new neurons in the brain, what is known in the field as "neurogenesis," can occur at anytime in response to our lived experience. How do neuroscientific researchers know this? Siegel notes that brain-imaging studies reveal new and increased neural activity in certain regions of the brain that correlates with "specific mental functions, such as focusing attention, recalling a past event, or feeling pain" (2011, p. 38–39). More specifically, the focusing of attention that correlates with an increase in neural activity occurs when we are engaged in contemplative-meditational practice. It is therefore becoming more common for brain-imaging to, in the words of the renowned neuropsychiatrist and Nobel laureate, Eric Kandel, "evaluate the metabolic activity of discrete regions of the brain while people are engaged in specific tasks under controlled conditions" (2013, p. 9). He observes from the growing body of neuroimaging research and findings that

> There is now considerable evidence for functional plasticity, at chemical synapses. Long-term changes (lasting days) can give rise to further physiological changes that lead to anatomical alterations, including pruning of preexisting synapses and even growth of new ones....Chemical synapses are functionally and anatomically modified through experience and learning as much as during early development (2013, p. 37).

The neuroscientific findings have important implications for the work of pastoral care and counseling in an age of increased anxiety, even more when they are juxtaposed with other neuroimaging studies. For example, Andrew Newberg's longitudinal study of Franciscan nuns engaged in the daily practice of Centering Prayer and Buddhist monks practicing mindfulness meditation has revealed, rather compellingly, the process of neuroplasticity in the context of contemplative spiritual practice. Newberg focused on particular regions of the brain for both the nuns and the monks, in particular the region most associated with arousal and stress, the amygdala. Located within the temporal lobe of the brain, the amygdala or "stress center" is a limbic-system structure that is involved in the activation and the processing of survival-based emotions such as fear and anxiety. While a certain amount of amygdala activity is of course necessary for human survival and even for daily human life, "an overly active limbic system, which generates our emotional states, is physically and psychologically dangerous" (Newberg, 2009, p. 50). The evidence from neuroimaging research, however, is revealing that daily contemplative spiritual practice, particularly mindfulness-based prayer and meditation, will in fact lower activity in the amygdala, calming the stress region of the brain. Newberg recounts the pivotal experience of studying "a group of nuns who had been practicing the Centering Prayer for a minimum of fifteen years":

> This was the first brain-scan study of Christian contemplative practitioners, and we discovered that the neurological changes were significant and very different from how the human brain normally functions. Even more surprising, the neurological changes were nearly the same as those we recorded from a group of Buddhist practitioners, who obviously nurtured very different beliefs. This evidence confirmed our hypothesis that the benefits gleaned from prayer and meditation may have less to do with a specific theology than with the ritual techniques of breathing, staying relaxed, and focusing one's attention upon a concept that evokes comfort, compassion, or a spiritual sense of peace. Of course, the more you believe in what you are meditating or praying about, the stronger the response will be (2009, p. 48).

While there is a growing interest in contemplative neuroscience, there are few resources that make the research from this emerging field accessible to and relevant for those engaged in the work of pastoral and spiritual care. It is important that those of us working in the field of pastoral care and counseling begin to bridge this gap by offering to clients and congregants specific methods to affect lasting and transformative changes in the mind and brain. This of course presupposes having a basic understanding of neuroplasticity and the promise it holds for human growth and development, both individually and collectively. The field of neuroscience helps us to see that the human brain is a remarkable "anticipation machine," always preparing for what comes next in the future based on what has happened to us in the past. Siegel likes to say that "neurons that fire together, wire together," meaning that as our lived experience becomes "encoded by the firing of neurons in groups," these neural clusters of memory will continue to be retrieved and further reinforced by "an internal event—a thought or feeling—or an external event that the brain associates in some way to a happening in the past" (2011, p. 148). Over time, we build up memory clusters that will size up the current situation of our lives in a split-second, what the cognitive neuroscientist would call the process of *automaticity*. "In this way the patterns we encode in memory actually bias our ongoing perceptions and change the way we interact with the world" (Siegel, 2011, p. 148). Sometimes, as we all know, this can be beneficial in our daily lives, other times less helpful as when anxious and fearful memory patterns are reactivated disproportionately in the context of everyday relational experiences by excessive amygdala activity. As any pastoral and clinical practitioner knows, human relationships are prone to emotional reactivity that is disproportionate to the current situation, driven by the encoded memory of a painful experience(s) in the past.

As we harness the power of mindful awareness, paying close attention to anxious memory patterns that fire automatically and involuntarily in response to events and situations in the present, we begin to develop an "observing self" that can monitor, modulate, and modify when necessary our internal states. Called mindfulness or mindful awareness, the technique involves observing one's "thoughts and feelings from the perspective of a nonjudgmental third party" (Davidson, 2012, p. 173). If, for example, an anxious thought or feeling arises, we do not at one extreme fight it nor do we at another extreme let it rule our experience; either way our experience becomes "hijacked" by anxious reactivity. According to Davidson, the "nonjudgmental" part of mindful awareness is key, for it helps us to develop a spacious awareness of the totality of our experience, observing the comings and goings of our thoughts and feelings "as just the exudations of [our] brain's synapses and action potentials" (2012, p. 201). Indeed, the focus of a new and potentially beneficial wave of therapeutic approaches, namely, mindfulness- and acceptance-based behavioral therapies, which we will explore in greater depth in later chapters, begins with helping clients "pay attention in the present moment to whatever arises internally or externally, without becoming entangled or 'hooked' by judging or wishing things were otherwise" (Roemer & Orsillo, 2009, p. 2). For the religious believer, getting "hooked" could take the form of fighting with her anxious thoughts and feelings, of reactively "siding" with her inner critic's accusations that a person of faith should trust in God and not feel anxious in the first place. Jesus, after all, encourages us not to be anxious about tomorrow, and while most of us, Christian or not, would support this as a foundational teaching for the spiritual life, there is less clarity about if and how it can actually be applied in the context of everyday life. The teaching is conveyed sermonically from the pulpit all the time that it is a sign of faith to trust in God and not live anxiously, but beyond the conceptual and intellectual grasp of Jesus' words there is less understanding of how to make this a practical reality. Additionally, the anxious congregant may feel guilty upon hearing these words for not having enough faith to quell her anxiety, and thus along with feeling anxious about balancing, for example, a career, a marriage, family obligations, and so forth she now feels anxious and guilty about feeling anxious. It is not that she is resisting the teaching to feel less anxious about her life and about tomorrow; rather, she does not know *how* to put the teaching into practice. The pastoral caregiver, beyond admonishing her not to feel anxious and instead trust in God, can now through the discovery of neuroplasticity offer specific ways to monitor and modulate her mind and brain in order to live more fully into Jesus' teaching.

In the context of mindfulness- and acceptance-based approaches to therapeutic care, it would mean helping the congregant or client to cultivate a compassionate and nonjudgmental stance toward his or her internal experiences (Roemer & Orsillo, 2009, p. 221), including any anxious thoughts and feelings, to simply notice and observe the totality of one's inner world. This has important implications for the spiritual life and our spiritual practices, for as we all know the minute we begin to meditate and pray, the internal chatter of the mind commences. "The worst thing you can do," Newberg points out, "is to critically judge your performance...self-criticism stimulates the amygdala, which releases myriad stress-provoking neurochemicals and hormones" (2009, p. 195). Put another way, the more we judge our meditational "performance" and how well we are doing, for example, whether we meditated long enough or should have given it a better effort, the more we feed and reinforce the powerful negativity bias of the brain. As Siegel observes, "our effort to combat our actual experience creates internal tension, a kind of self-inflicted stress" (2011, p. 97). Thus, whether we engage in a contemplative-meditational practice for ten or fifteen minutes a day or an hour, it becomes more valuable, neurologically and I would argue spiritually, if it is practiced with a minimum of self-critique. Obviously, the longer we can engage in daily spiritual practices, the more neurological changes will occur in the brain. That said, a regular meditational practice of even ten or fifteen minutes a day will also foster neuroplasticity over time. What is most fundamental is that one's specific approach to prayer and meditation, however long and in whatever shape and form it ultimately takes, become a *daily* practice. Newberg's studies reveal that "five minutes of prayer once a week may have little effect, but forty minutes of daily practice, over a period of years, will bring permanent changes to the brain" (2009, p. 195).

As those in our care develop an observing self to monitor internal and reactive states of fear and anxiety, they are better able to make fuller use of daily spiritual practices that have the capacity to, in the words of Siegel, "decouple automaticity, awaken the mind, and create the essential pause of emotional and social intelligence" (2010, p. 229). More fundamentally, this creates and infuses the present moment with what the Buddhist psychologist and teacher Tara Brach would call a *sacred pause:* "When we are caught up in striving and obsessing and leaning into the future, [a sacred pause] enables us to reenter the mystery and vitality only found here and now" (Brach, 2003, p. 71). The pastoral practitioner, equipped with some understanding of neuroscientific findings, can begin to situate the care of souls within a therapeutic framework that will "provide an important context for understanding not only the nature of religious and spiritual practices, but *how* (italics mine) such practices have a direct impact on health and well being" (Newberg, 2010, p. 205). To be sure, the field of contemplative neuroscience can offer us a more precise understanding of not only *what* Jesus teaches in the Sermon on the Mount but even more *how* to make his teaching a practical reality in everyday life. As pastoral caregivers and clinical practitioners become more knowledgeable of neuroscientific studies and research, such as the finding that contemplative prayer and meditation can potentially lower amygdala activity in the brain and by extension our level of stress and anxiety, we can help to educate those in our care about the practical benefits of a daily spiritual practice. I will have much more to say about this in later chapters.

USING THE MIND TO REWIRE THE BRAIN

Before going any further, it is worth noting that some readers, even professional caregivers and clinical practitioners, may feel some uneasiness at the thought of holding in tension, correlationally and dialectically, brain science and the core of the Judeo-Christian faith tradition. Historically, religion and science have not always been the best conversation partners, nor have they always been on speaking terms. The theologian Ian Barbour, in his classic book, *Religion and Science* (1997), has identified four historical methods of relating science and religion: (1) *conflict*, where there is often a war between scientific materialism and biblical literalism; (2) *independence*, with science and religion keeping their distance from each other, reverting to their own separate methodological corners of inquiry; (3) *dialogue*, where the two engage in meaningful conversation, although at the end of the day they are still very much ensconced in their own paradigmatic frameworks; and (4) *integration* that goes beyond mere dialogue toward collaborative, bi-directional, and reciprocal learning. The latter approaches to science and religion, "dialogue" and "integration," I would argue are in keeping with Tillich's correlational method, where pastoral practitioners, in Tillich's words, actually *use* the immense and profound material of the existential analysis in *all* cultural realms, including science in general and more specifically the growing body of neuroscientific research and evidence. A statement widely attributed to St. Augustine is that all truth, wherever it is located, is God's truth, whether it be found in the church, a theological treatise, a science lab, a brain-imaging scan, and so on ad infinitum. If we put it in the words of the psalmist, we can say, similarly, that the earth, or more accurately the universe is God's and the fullness thereof, the universe and *all* that is therein (Psalm 24:1).

Still, even to this day there exists at times a certain amount of conflict between science and religion, and this is no different when it comes to brain science, which may give some pause to going any further. Scientific materialism remains quite popular, paradigmatically, with the view that all there is in the universe, including human life and consciousness, is reducible to matter and energy. In the context of neuroscience, the materialist view would hold that certain constructs, such as mind and consciousness, are reducible to neurochemical events in the brain, nothing less and certainly nothing more. What exists inside the human skull is therefore a three-pound mass of fatty tissue, quite remarkable in and of itself, but this does not in any way suggest the existence of other non-materialist realities such as mind and consciousness let alone that there is a spiritual dimension to human life. Simply put, "from the materialist perspective, our human mind's consciousness and free will are problems to be explained away" (Beauregard, 2007, p. xi), all reducible to the neural and synaptic activity occurring in the brain. It would be quite understandable, then, if some readers of this book who embrace a more non-materialistic perspective would feel some tension at the thought of correlating the findings of neuroscience with the core of their religious faith and belief system. I would simply encourage a temporary suspension of judgment, at least for some Judeo-Christian readers and practitioners, a temporary bracketing of their assumptions about the materialistic bent of science in general and neuroscience in particular. This is not meant to obscure or minimize the "dominance of materialism in neuroscience today":

> Materialists think that the distinction you make between your mind as an
> immaterial entity and your brain as a bodily organ has no real basis. The mind
> is assumed to be a mere illusion generated by the workings of the brain. Some
> materialists even think you should not in fact *use* terminology that implies that
> your mind exists (Beauregard, 2007, p. x).

There are other researchers, however, who take a broader view, one that is
less dogmatic and more open to non-materialist perspectives and to collaborative and reciprocal, i.e., *integrative* learning with contemplative traditions
of religious and spiritual practice. Dogmatism and hubris, to be sure, can be
and are found anywhere and everywhere within the vast array of human
experience and investigation, certainly within religion but also at times within the scientific community. It is important that pastoral and spiritual practitioners, seeking to find more effective ways to care for anxious clients and
congregants, not look beyond the findings of neuroscience simply because of
the materialism dominating the field. There are other scientists, for example,
the researcher Richard Davidson working in the area of contemplative neuroscience, who intentionally incorporate the wisdom of diverse fields and disciplines into their methodological framework, who are not satisfied with an
exclusive materialist epistemology. Davidson, along with another renowned
colleague, Jon Kabat-Zinn, an expert in medical science and meditational
practice, point out that "an extraordinary confluence of epistemologies, or
different ways of knowing, is unfolding in the present era" (2011a, p. 1). This
presupposes that a single way of knowing, whether it be scientific or religious, cannot fully capture the wide range of human life and experience, for
the vastness and complexity of God's creation and universe defies any singu-
lar and totalizing explanation. As Hamlet once famously said to his friend,
"There are more things in heaven and earth, Horatio, than are dreamt of in
your philosophy" (Shakespeare, 1978, 1.5.166–167). Collaborative dialogue
and integration, not to mention a modicum of humility, is necessary for
grasping more comprehensively the "things in heaven and earth" and what
constitutes the fullness of human life and experience. The specific confluence or convergence that Davidson and Kabat-Zinn are referring to is that of
neuroscience with the contemplative-meditational traditions, which of course
will represent very different epistemologies—"different ways of investigat-
ing, explaining, and ultimately shaping human experience and our relationship to the larger world we find ourselves embedded in." They elaborate by
noting that

> In the case of the contemplative traditions, the vector of inquiry and investiga-
> tion up to now has been primarily inward directed, probing the domain of the
> mind. Yet until recently, interior experience was dismissed in some academic
> circles as merely "subjective," as opposed to "objective." Now it is getting a
> second look as an essential and valid phenomenological dimension of human

experience and knowing. …Since nothing in science to date actually explains the nature of our interior experience, it seems prudent to at least entertain the possibility that a systematic investigation of inner experience from the first-person perspective has its own valid parameters as an epistemology, and has the potential (especially coupled with third-person methodologies) to contribute profoundly to a balanced and collaborative investigation of what we call the mind and human experience, including the dilemmas of suffering, greed, aggression, delusion, and ignorance, the tyranny and dangers inherent in Socrates' "unexamined life"—the mind that, contrary to the appellation *Homo sapiens sapiens,* does not know itself. This is the very much alive and relevant arena of the contemplative traditions, what might be called their "laboratory domain" (2011a, pp. 2–3).

While a materialist paradigm continues to dominate the sciences, including that of the human brain, increasingly there are neuroscientific investigators and researchers who are quite interested in and committed to the convergence of scientific and contemplative-meditational epistemologies and ways of knowing. In theological terms, it represents a correlational approach that is collaborative, dialogical, and integrative in nature, a methodological stance that intentionally represents bi-directional and reciprocal learning. As such, a "non-materialist neuroscience is not compelled to reject, deny, explain away, or treat as problems all evidence that defies materialism," which, as Mario Beauregard notes in *The Spiritual Brain*, "is promising because current research is turning up a growing body of such evidence" (2007, p. xiv). For example, what is emerging from a collaborative investigation of interior experience or what we would call *mind*, between non-materialist neuroscience and religious and spiritual traditions, is an increasing knowledge of the importance and necessity of daily contemplative-meditational practice. It has even led noted neuroscientific researchers like Jeffrey Schwartz (2003) and Rick Hanson (2009) to put forward, respectively, the practical benefits of self-directed neuroplasticity and the practical neuroscience of happiness, love, and wisdom. In so doing, "non-materialist approaches to the mind result in practical benefits and treatments, as well as promising approaches to phenomena that materialist accounts cannot even address" (Beauregard, 2007, p. xvi). The relevance for pastoral and spiritual care becomes more obvious, as we seek to develop very precise methods geared toward the effective care and support of clients and congregants. What we are learning from non-materialist studies is that we and those in our care can use the mind to rewire and change the brain, incrementally of course from day to day yet over time in profound and lasting ways. Through collaborative engagement with non-materialist neuroscience, providers of pastoral and spiritual care will discover, correlationally, that contemplative, meditational, and mystical experience from various religious and spiritual traditions "indicates that the nature of mind, consciousness, and reality as well as the meaning of life can be apprehended through an intuitive, unitive, and experiential form of knowing" (Beauregard, 2007, p. 294).

Certainly, this presupposes a basic understanding of the human *mind*, that it is a reality unto itself and not synonymous with the human *brain*. Siegel writes that "the mind can be defined, in part, as an embodied and relational process that regulates the flow of energy and information" (2010, p. 25). It therefore has a regulatory function that monitors and modifies when necessary the flow of energy and information within oneself and relationally between people. This process of monitoring and modifying reflects the harnessed power of mindful awareness, a prerequisite to rewiring and changing the brain. "One of the key practical lessons of modern neuroscience is that the power to direct our attention has within it the power to shape our brain's firing patterns, as well as the architecture of the brain itself" (Siegel, 2011, p. 39). But again this assumes the existence of another reality above and beyond the biological brain, which is mind and consciousness. Moreover, for the pastoral caregiver and pastoral counselor, we can also add to mind and consciousness another reality, namely, the existence of spirit that is, to be sure, connected to the biological brain but is not limited or reducible to it. This is a matter of the utmost practical importance for pastoral and spiritual practitioners, for time and again we see that "when spiritual experiences transform lives, the most reasonable explanation and the one that best accounts for all the evidence, is that the people who have such experiences have actually contacted a reality outside themselves, a reality that has brought them closer to the real nature of the universe" (Beauregard, 2007, p. xvi). The science of the human brain, even that of a materialist perspective, correlates in many ways with pastoral theology and pastoral practice, yet in other ways it is limited when it puts forward a myopic and perhaps dogmatic view of life, the world, and the universe. Echoing the words of Hamlet, pastoral theology affirms that we live in a rather big and mysterious universe, that there is more in heaven and earth, including mind, consciousness, and spirit than can ever be dreamt of by human beings in our philosophy, theology, and science.

Self-directed neuroplasticity or the practical neuroscience of helping those in our care monitor and modulate their anxiety and stress in order to live more joyfully and peacefully, presupposes the existence of something other than objective material reality, namely, subjective experience. Siegel notes that while he is certainly informed by neuroscientific studies and research, he is also as a clinician fully steeped in the inner subjective world. "Our internal world is real," he writes in *The Mindful Brain*, "though it may not be quantifiable in ways that science often requires for careful analysis" (2007, p. xviii). The inner world of human subjectivity cannot therefore be reduced to nothing more than the neural activity and functioning of the biological brain or, in the words of Richard Davidson, to "the three pounds of tofulike tissue we call the brain" (2012, p. 136). Siegel adds that "this internal world, this subjective stuff of mind, is at the heart of what enables us to sense each other's pain, to embrace each other at times of distress, to revel in each other's joy, to create meaning in the stories of our lives, to find connection in each other's eyes" (2007, pp. xviii–xix). This is the embodied and relational nature of mind and brain, which reflects the network or system of "mirror neurons" so vital for social cognition and intelligence. Human relationships are indeed "woven into the fabric of our interior world" to the extent that "our awareness of another person's state of mind depends on how well we know our own" (Siegel, 2011, pp. 62–63). This again assumes the existence of another reality above and beyond that of objective material reality, namely, the world of subjective experience, although the two worlds, objectivity and subjectivity, are never entirely separate or independent from each other.

While our experience of mind cannot be located, like the brain, in a precise physical location, it nevertheless exists in time. For example, "when I say a scene is 'breathtaking,' I refer to my subjective experience of the scene, not the particular activation of my visual cortex" (Barrett, 2011, p. 17). Or, that I feel anxious and fearful this particular moment reflects my inner subjective experience of an objective brain state, the fact that neural circuits connected to my amygdala are activated and firing. By taking as our fundamental starting point the view that the physical objective world *coexists* with the inner subjective world, that "what they share in common is a co-occurrence in time," we can, according to Siegel, "find a new way of looking at this old question":

> To look at this problem from a different angle, it is helpful to clarify some basic ideas. The experiential, subjective side of reality is non-objective in that you could not weigh it, hold it in your hand, or capture the subjective nature of such inner experiences with a camera—not even with a functional brain-imaging scanner. This inner world, the subjective essence of our mental life, is not the same as brain activity. We may ascertain that in the moment of time when we sense fear we can also capture on a computerized scan an assembled technical image that the amygdala is becoming active in the limbic region of our brain. But notice how in truth we can only say that the physical firing and the subjective experience occur virtually at the same time: the amygdala firing is not the same as feeling fear. We need to keep an open mind about the direction of causal influences: imagining fear may induce the amygdala to become active as much as the amygdala becoming active "gives us" the feeling of fear. …If the answer to the issue of brain and mind were as unidirectional as the common statement, "the mind is just the activity of the brain," then there would not be much more to talk about. Your brain will take care of everything. The natural implication would be that we are slaves to our brain. But findings from science now confirm the notion that the mind can activate the brain's circuitry in ways that change the brain's structural connections. In

other words, you can use the subjective inner aspect of reality to alter the objective physical structure of the brain (2010, pp. 6–7).

The potential for self-directed neuroplasticity holds great promise for personal growth, development, and healing, for relational attunement in the context of marriage, family life, and social relations, and for the work of pastoral and spiritual care. Our subjective experience of mind reveals that as we and those in our care stimulate the firing of neurons in the brain through mental activity and training and through the daily practice of contemplative prayer and meditation, the same neurons will wire together in ways that foster health and well-being. Communication between mind and brain is therefore not unidirectional, as if it stems from neurochemical activity in the brain alone. "If we make causal phrases like this, the erroneous idea is reinforced that the mind is only created by the brain," whereas "the directional arrow goes both ways: the mind can actually use the brain to create itself" (Siegel, 2007, p. 48). In other words, communication between mind and brain is bi-directional and reciprocal, a two-way street as it were. Mental activity and training, including in particular the spiritual practices of mindfulness meditation and contemplative prayer, stimulates brain firing as much as the firing of neurons stimulates mental activity. This harks back to Siegel's statement that neurons that we intentionally fire together will wire together accordingly, a form of "brain hygiene" or fitness that creates and strengthens neural connections and groupings. Just as we would intentionally activate and flex other muscles of the body when working out in the gym, "we can focus our minds to build the specific 'muscle groups' of the brain, reinforcing their connections, establishing new circuitry, and linking them together in new and helpful ways" (Siegel, 2011, p. 40).

As we learn to carefully train the mind in order to wire and rewire the neural connections and synaptic linkages in the brain, we find that there is the potential for personal and relational growth and transformation. "Mental activity," writes Davidson, "ranging from meditation to cognitive-behavior therapy, can alter brain function in specific circuits, with the result that you can develop a broader awareness of social signals, a deeper sensitivity to your own feelings and bodily sensations, and a more consistently positive outlook" (2012, p. 11). Recall that the human mind is fundamentally a relational and embodied process that regulates the flow of energy and information, thus enabling us to monitor and modify if necessary certain patterns of unhelpful and unproductive brain activity, e.g., excessive worrying and rumination. Put another way, "mind is not 'just' brain activity; energy and information flow happens in a brain within the body and it happens in relationships" (Siegel, 2007, p. 49). Siegel, revealing more of his interpersonal-neurobiology framework, rhetorically asks in *Mindsight*, what is it that is being monitored and then modified by the mind, as a regulatory process? He answers the question by suggesting that

> The mind observes information and energy flow and then shapes the characteristics, patterns, and direction of the flow. Each of us has a unique mind: unique thoughts, feelings, perceptions, memories, beliefs, and attitudes, and a unique set of regulatory patterns. These patterns shape the flow of energy and information inside us, and we also share them with other minds. ...When I say the mind is *embodied*, I mean that the regulation of energy and information flow happens, in part, in the body. It occurs where we usually imagine our mental life taking place, in the circuits and synapses of the brain, inside the skull. But it also occurs throughout the body, in the distributed nervous system, which monitors and influences energy and information flowing through our heart and our intestines, and even shapes the activity of our immune system. Finally, the mind is a *relational* process. Energy and information flow between and among people, and they are monitored and modified in this shared exchange. . . . Relationships are the way we share energy and information flow, and it is this sharing that shapes, in part, how the flow is regulated. Our minds are created within relationships—including the one we have with ourselves (2011, pp. 54–55).

INCREMENTAL ALTERATIONS IN NEURAL STRUCTURE

For pastoral and clinical practitioners working in an age of heightened anxiety, it is necessary to have a basic understanding of neuroplasticity and how it can be, to a certain extent, self-directed by using the mind to change the brain. And the best means of doing so is through the daily practice of contemplative prayer and mindfulness meditation. It is equally important to understand that a daily spiritual practice must be cultivated over time and even then there is no ironclad guarantee and promise that we will never again feel anxious or fall back into old patterns of negativity and reactivity. In other words, the promise of neuroplasticity fostered by daily contemplative-meditational practice is not another quick-fix strategy to be added to the already voluminous self-help literature. Nor is it, as we will see, an avoidance of the difficulties of life, the so-called "shadow side" of human experience. Rather, the promise of neuroplasticity assumes a mindful awareness of the totality of life, one's own and that of others, a deeply spiritual undertaking to be cultivated with great care and patience throughout the entire lifespan. But using the mind to change the brain runs counter to the ingrained negativity bias of the brain and its predisposition to be anxious and alert at all times, something that we will address more in-depth in the next chapter. We are first and foremost hardwired for survival and therefore have an evolutionary predisposition to feel anxious, preempting pain and suffering by remaining vigilant and on high alert even in the most ordinary circumstances of everyday life.

"This state of affairs," writes Joseph LeDoux in *Synaptic Self*, "is part of the price we pay for having newly evolved cognitive capacities that are not yet fully integrated into our brains" (2002, p. 322). Thus, while the good news is that awareness of the reality of neuroplasticity and the importance of cultivating a mindful approach to external and internal experience is generally on the rise in Western culture, along with the implications for personal and relational growth and transformation, the more sobering bit of news is that in our attempts to rewire mind and brain we are going against powerful ancient currents lodged within the central nervous system (Hanson, 2009, p. 46).

The starting point for such a paradigmatic turn toward contemplative neuroscience in the field of pastoral and spiritual care is therefore an acknowledgment of the brain's negativity bias, and as we will see in chapter three, how certain Judeo-Christian beliefs and doctrines have the potential to inadvertently reinforce the bias and thwart our attempts to live more joyfully and peacefully. More specifically, the "negativity bias" may be defined as the brain's capacity to detect negative information faster than positive information, to recognize and recall with more intensity painful circumstances than pleasant and even joyful experiences. Throughout human history, the negativity bias of the brain has served an evolutionary purpose that motivates us to avoid danger and to anticipate potential threats to our individual and collective survival. We are therefore primed to approach life with a certain anxious and defensive predisposition, exaggerating negative information about life events and human relationships while downplaying positive experiences. Keeping in mind Jesus' foundational teaching from the Sermon on the Mount, we are able to see that while it is in our best interests not to be anxious about the future, we are neurologically hardwired to approach life with a certain vigilance and anxious awareness. For most people, it is the "normal baseline" state of the brain even at rest, a lurking background feeling of alertness that keeps us vigilant and on edge. Brain-scan research has revealed that, in the words of neuropsychologist Rick Hanson, the "brain is like Velcro for negative experiences and Teflon for positive ones—even though most of our experiences are probably neutral or positive" (2009, p. 41). The deeply ingrained negativity bias, once necessary for our moment-to-moment survival, is often excessive for human life in today's world, so much so that researchers into marriage and human relationships have found that it takes at least five positive affirmations and interactions to balance the overvaluation of a single negative experience (Gottman, 1995, p. 57). Because the brain is still very much hardwired to protect us from potential danger and pain at all costs, it is important to remember, as Bruce McEwen points out in *The End of Stress as We Know It*, that the "bad stuff" still has priority and will continue to for the foreseeable future: "Messages of love, reassurance, courage, and hope can almost certainly influence the body as well but not with the same galvanic effect" (2002, p. 149).

Siegel himself with a touch of humor, although probably not so humorous at the time, recounts a personal experience where he was hijacked by powerful undercurrents of anxiety, frustration, and stress at the sight of his thirteen-year-old son and nine-year-old daughter squabbling over a crepe after watching a movie. His son was already eating a crepe, Siegel offered to order one for his daughter, but his daughter only wanted part of her brother's. And, as the story goes, the son steadfastly refused to share even a bite with his sister. Recalling this challenging moment in the life of his family, Siegel refers to it as the "crepes of wrath":

> I was about to explode. When the bantering continued, something inside of me shifted. My head began to spin, but I told myself that I would remain calm and appeal to reason. I could feel my face tense up, my fists get taut, and my heart begin to beat faster, but I tried to ignore these signals. That was it for me. Feeling overwhelmed by the ridiculousness of the whole encounter, I got up, took my daughter's hand, and went outside to wait on the sidewalk in front of the shop until my son had finished his crepe. A few minutes later he emerged and asked why we had left. As I stormed off toward the car, my daughter in tow and my son hurrying to keep up, I told them that they should learn to share their food with each other…by then I was boiling over with frustration and at that point there was no turning off the heat…We got to the car and, fired up, I ignited the engine and away we went for home. They had been normal siblings out for movies and a snack. I became a father out of his mind (2011, pp. 23–25).

Siegel, one of the foremost experts in the science and practice of mindfulness, attempted to override the hyperactivity of the amygdala in the moment by appealing to reason, but to no avail. "Under certain crepelike conditions," he later recalls, "the 'limbic lava' from the fiery emotional centers below the cortex, just beneath the middle prefrontal area, can explode in out-of-control activity" (2011, p. 26).

This serves as something of a reality check for pastoral and clinical practitioners, lest we assume and convey to those in our care that the promise of neuroplasticity through contemplative-meditational practice is the path to a quick and permanent "fix" of long-established thought and memory patterns. We come into this world already possessing a negative predisposition toward life, the result of our evolutionary and biological hardwiring, and throughout our lives, particularly during the formative years of life, the negativity bias gets further reinforced by anxious and reactive patterns that become deeply encoded in our memory. As we learn from Siegel's research and from the account of his own personal experience, these anxious and fearful memory patterns, reactivated and driven by heightened amygdala activity, continue to resurface in any given moment and impact and bias the way we interact with the world and those around us, even those we care about the most. Without

an active and ongoing spiritual practice to balance our anxious and reactive
memory patterns, the negativity bias of the brain will continue to have the
upper hand. It has been said that we are what we eat. In this case, we are what
we feed the mind and the brain. "The more we anxiously tell ourselves
stories about how we might fail or what is wrong with us or with others, the
more we deepen the grooves—the neural pathways—that generate feelings
of deficiency" (Brach, 2003, p. 17). As Mario Beauregard explains, the more
we engage in and reinforce any repetitive thought or memory pattern, "the
more neurons are drawn into it" and the stronger the firing pattern becomes.
He adds, metaphorically:

> What was once a neural footpath slowly grows into a twelve-lane highway
> whose deafening traffic takes over the neural neighborhood. The challenge is
> to return it to the status of a footpath in the brain again. Neuroplasticity (the
> ability of neurons to shift their connections and responsibilities) makes that
> possible (2007, p. 128).

Neuroscience has demonstrated quite remarkably in recent years that the
plasticity and malleability of the brain is indeed a potential reality, fostered in
particular by the *daily* spiritual practice of mindfulness meditation and/or
contemplative prayer. The static view of the brain has steadily been sup-
planted by a much more dynamic picture, to the extent that it can now be said
with no shortage of confidence that "the brain is an extraordinarily plastic
biological system that is in a state of dynamic equilibrium with the external
world" (Ramachandran, 2011, p. 37). This important and timely discovery,
as we have been noting, will increasingly have profound implications and
relevance for pastoral and spiritual care in today's world as congregants and
clients seek specific ways to manage their stress and anxiety more effectively
and in so doing to feel less overwhelmed by the exigencies of contemporary
life. As Siegel's slice-of-life example illustrates, the process of "resculpting"
the neural grooves and pathways of the brain through contemplative-meditational practice *must* become a regular practice if we are to turn the noisy
neural highway, so often amygdala-driven, into a more peaceful and tranquil
footpath. Each time we pause in our daily spiritual practice to harness the
power of mindful awareness and infuse positive thoughts and feelings and
views into anxious memory patterns and limiting states of mind, we build a
small amount of new neural structure. "Over time," notes Hanson, "the accumulating impact of this positive material will literally, synapse by synapse,
change your brain" (2009, p. 71).

The building up of new neural structure was what was occurring with the
Franciscan nuns in Newberg's study, after engaging in the Centering Prayer
for fifteen or more years. Over time, this daily spiritual practice of carefully
focusing the attention on a sacred word or mantra created the necessary space

where neuroplasticity was fostered by enhancing the structural growth of neural connections and synaptic linkages. Day after day and week after week, "the results are tiny, incremental alterations in neural structure that add up as the years go by" (Hanson, 2009, p. 72). The evidence from neuroscientific research strongly suggests that "by repeated thoughts and actions we can alter not only the functioning but also the structure of the neural networks in our brains" (McEwen, 2002, p. 149), which means that each time we engage in contemplative prayer and meditation we are literally rewiring synaptic connections and "re-sculpting" neural pathways. We are also calming the limbic region of the brain by lowering the activity of the amygdala, a fundamental prerequisite to feeling less anxious about tomorrow. The daily practice of contemplative prayer and meditation makes, as McEwen observes, "a minute but long-term, possibly permanent, change in our brains":

> The more synapses are dedicated to an experience, the more likely that experience is to become a permanent feature in the memory's landscape. Imagine a trail through the woods. The more hikers that walk on it, the more deeply it will be imprinted on the forest floor (2002, pp. 120 & 149).

Chapter Two

A Built-In Negativity Bias

I will praise thee; for I am fearfully and wonderfully made: marvelous are thy works; and that my soul knoweth right well. —Psalm 139:14 (KJV)

The discovery of the plasticity of the human brain holds great promise for the practice of pastoral and spiritual care, provided we understand that this is never reducible to a simple self-help or quick-fix strategy. As we noted earlier, the promise of neuroplasticity presupposes an understanding of the brain's hardwired bias toward negative thoughts, feelings, experiences, memories, and so forth. This "negativity bias" reflects the brain's capacity to scan for and detect negative information more quickly than positive information, to maximize and exaggerate the former while minimizing and downplaying the latter. "There are some things," writes the cognitive neuroscientist, Michael Gazzaniga, "that affect us in a positive manner, although there is no equivalent to the emergency status given to negative stimuli" (2008, p. 123). Indeed, we have learned that the brain is like Velcro for negative and unpleasant experiences, real and/or imagined, whereas it is like Teflon for those that are more positive. "Consequently, even when positive experiences outnumber negative ones, the pile of negative implicit memories naturally grows faster" (Hanson, 2009, p. 68). Like Velcro, unpleasant and painful experiences and memories "stick" to and with the brain more deeply and lastingly, and therefore are recalled with more galvanic force and resonance than joyful and even uplifting experiences. It is, to be sure, the price we pay for our present level of collective human development, which is a reminder that rewiring the brain happens incrementally throughout the entire lifespan and never overnight. How far we can go with the neural rewiring of the brain and to what extent we can change it ultimately remains a mystery, because at the present moment neuroscience does "not know how much plasticity the

27

emotional brain is capable of" (Davidson, 2012, p. 226). On the one hand, every time we engage in contemplative-meditational practice to harness the power of mindful awareness and infuse positive feelings into negative memory patterns, we build new neural structure that over time will clearly change our brain. On the other hand, the negativity bias so deeply embedded in the brain reveals that at least for the time being "there are limits to the range one can travel" (Davidson, 2012, p. 226).

THE NAGGINGS OF PESSIMISM

In a conversation with the Dalai Lama at the 2005 conference of the *Mind and Life Institute* held in Washington, DC, the noted researcher Wolf Singer pointed out that from a neurobiological perspective "our brains are the product of an evolutionary process, arranged through trial and error and adapted to our world" (2011, p. 186). Over millennia, the brain has built up neural structure geared toward the continuation of the human race and species, methods of survival that are intended to maintain and preserve our existence individually and collectively. These survival strategies become encoded as templates in the brain, helping us to anticipate and predict future scenarios in a split second. "Our brains," according to Singer, "have implemented pragmatic strategies of survival to keep the organisms that possess them alive in a world that is full of uncertainties and dangers" (2011, p. 186). This, of course, further reinforces the neurological predisposition toward negativity, which has developed out of necessity from time immemorial for our human good and survival. The negativity bias is therefore part and parcel of every human being's experience, and will continue to be for the foreseeable future. Thus, for pastoral and spiritual caregivers, it is important to keep in mind that the baseline for health and well-being is not the eradication of something that is so deeply embedded in our human neurology, i.e., the brain's predisposition toward negativity, but rather the mindful monitoring and modulation of anxious thoughts and feelings. "What our brains are driven to do is make models of the world to derive predictions for further action," such as "it is better to know when the tiger is coming than to be surprised and get eaten" (Singer, 2011, p. 186).

We have already noted that a contemplative style of life and spiritual practice in many ways runs counter to the fearful and vigilant currents that are more deeply lodged in the central nervous system. For as Hanson points out, "it goes against the evolutionary template to undo the causes of suffering, to feel one with all things, to flow with the changing moment, and to remain unmoved by pleasant and unpleasant alike" (2009, p. 46). It also goes against the evolutionary template to follow the Sermon-on-the-Mount teaching, to focus less and not more on tomorrow and the next day, to be less anxious and vigilant about the future. In terms of the human brain's present level of development, we could even go so far as to say that what Jesus is asking of us is not natural or "normal." Rather, the negativity bias and predis position of the brain is a reminder that, at least for the time being, the normal baseline of the brain, even at rest, is anxious awareness. For practitioners and those in our care, it is important not to forget that the path of increasing mindful and non-anxious awareness will feel, at least at the present moment of our collective human development, somewhat counterintuitive and perhaps a bit "unnatural." And yet, neuroscientific studies are revealing that we can indeed begin to change or rewire our brains incrementally, that a daily contemplative-meditational practice will help us lessen our anxious awareness by restraining "emotional reactions that worked well on the Serengeti" and "beliefs that once helped us survive" (Hanson, 2009, p. 46).

Recognizing and understanding the brain's predisposition toward negativity and watchfulness will serve as a reality check in the practice of pastoral and spiritual care as well as the clinical practice of pastoral counseling and psychotherapy. Any pastoral and/or clinical practitioner knows firsthand that congregants and clients will sometimes harbor unrealistic expectations about the change process. Sometimes, individuals will assume that change is simply a matter of the will and therefore by willing change in one's personal life it is hoped that immediately following the pastoral care or counseling session or by tomorrow at the latest change will be a fait accompli. In my own pastoral and clinical practice, a frequent intervention I like to make is to reframe the process of change as something that goes against the grain of accumulated formative experiences and runs counter to certain thought and memory patterns built up over time. For example, with a fifty-year-old client who is frustrated that change sometimes feels so elusive and ephemeral, I will try to convey empathically that since it has taken her fifty years to become who she is, she would do well to be patient and understanding and even compassionate with herself, to give herself a little time as she goes about the process of making substantive and lasting changes in her life. As Archie Smith and Ursula Riedel-Pfaefflin have noted, "how pastoral care providers account for human change will depend, in part, on what role living human systems as biological structures play in their explanation of change," which helps us better understand and appreciate "why change is complex, difficult to achieve, and hard to sustain" (2004, p. 79). In the context of this particular chapter, the specific biological structures that help us develop a more realistic understanding of the process of change and ultimately what can thwart it is the brain's center of gravity: a bias and predisposition toward negativity. Perhaps this is what St. Paul, the apostle of the apostles, is describing when he laments in his epistle to the Romans that he does not always do what he wants to do, and what he does not want to do he keeps on doing (Romans 7:15).

Changing the negative predisposition of the brain will take time, a life-time in fact, for in so doing we are swimming against powerful ancient currents of anxious and vigilant awareness that have helped human beings survive for millennia. On the one hand, the good news as we learned from Siegel in the last chapter is that neuroplasticity is always available to us and can occur across the lifespan. However, on the other hand, human beings have an ingrained predisposition to worry about tomorrow and to be anxious about the future, even those of us who live more optimistically. We need only recall the last time we awoke in the middle of the night and had difficul-ty getting back to sleep. "Worries that you easily dismiss during the day," writes the psychologist and founder of Positive Psychology, Martin Selig-man, "now overwhelm you: The argument with your spouse means divorce, the frown from the boss means you will be fired" (1990, p. 114). This "neurological turbulence" has "evolved to protect us in environments that were much more dangerous than anything most of us face today" (Hanson, 2009, pp. 164 & 170), and therefore it reflects not only the brain's inherent negativity bias but also and perhaps more powerful its predisposition to keep us alive at all costs. Seligman captures rather well the present stage of our collective human development:

> Evolution, however, has also given us our ancestors' Pleistocene brain. Through it come the naggings of pessimism: Success is fleeting; danger lurks around the next corner; tragedy awaits us; optimism is hubris. But the brain that accurately mirrored the grim realities of the ice ages now lags behind the less grim realities of modern life. Agriculture, and then the leap of industrial technology, put human beings in developed countries much less at the mercy of the next harsh winter. No longer do two out of three of our children die before they reach their fifth birthday. No longer is it reasonable for a woman to expect her own death during childbirth. No longer does massive starvation follow prolonged cold or drought. Certainly modern life has its own abundant menaces and tragedies: crime, AIDS, divorce, the threat of nuclear war, the undermining of the ecosystem. But it is only the most willfully negative ma-nipulation of the statistics that has modern life in the West even approach the level of disaster that shaped the ice-age brain. And so we do well to recognize the insistent voice of pessimism for the vestige it is (1990, p. 114).

Each of us is the bearer of the vestiges of the ice-age brain, which evolved in the context of a rather grim and dangerous age of human existence. Addition-ally, we all bear the vestiges of a brain that mirrors the grim and desperate and even terrifying realities of more recent times. Following the collapse of the Roman Empire, for example, much of Europe fell into a prolonged period of chaos and devastation, which required constant vigilant awareness from people of all classes in order to survive. Peasants across the continent would routinely huddle together in hamlets and villages, united by incessant fear as bands of raiders and marauders, real and imagined, threatened all semblance of peaceful existence. In order to have a moment's peace and quiet, and sometimes to get the slightest bit of sleep, it was not uncommon for these villagers to resort to excessive drinking to calm the ever present "night terrors." Commenting on Thomas Cahill's classic, *How the Irish Saved Civilization*, the reviewer Richard Bernstein (1995) notes that oftentimes the inhabitants of Ireland during the early Middle Ages, "while carefree and warlike on the outside, lived in 'quaking fear' within, their terror of shape-changing monsters, of sudden death and the insubstantiality of their world so acute that they drank themselves into an insensate stupor in order to sleep." And the Europe of the later Middle Ages continued with no shortage of grim realities and its share of acute threats and terrors. One can only wonder what it took for the average peasant to survive, physically and psychologically, the combinational force of a Hundred Years' War exacerbated by the sudden appearance of the Black Death. The impact of a war fought on and off over a century compounded by a series of deadly plagues was devastating to society, the economy, and to human life. In terms of the Black Death alone, the loss of human life staggers the imagination:

> The Black Death of 1348 and 1349, and the recurrent epidemics of the fourteenth and fifteenth centuries, were the most devastating natural disasters ever to strike Europe. We cannot cite exact losses; there are no global figures. The populations of some cities and villages, in areas as far removed from each other as England and Italy, fell in the late decades of the fourteenth century by 70 or 80 percent. The more we learn of the late medieval collapse in human numbers, the more awesome it appears. Europe in 1420 could have counted barely more than a third of the people it contained one hundred years before...the epidemics of modern history seem mild when compared with the fury of the Black Death (Herlihy, 1997, p. 17).

THE EMOTIONAL WARNING CENTER

Whether it is the vestige of human life and survival on the Serengeti, facing the grim realities of the ice age, the struggle to survive the terrifying realities of life following the collapse of Western civilization, and/or the impact of perpetual war punctuated and compounded by deadly plagues and epidemics, the reality is that the brain, individual and collective, does not soon or ever forget the accumulation of these difficult and in many cases traumatic experiences. As the work of Gerald May has revealed in the context of the treatment of addictions, the human brain with its billions of neurons and trillions of synaptic linkages between neurons "never completely forgets what it has learned" (1991, p. 90). And throughout the course of human history, one of the central learnings has been to remain preemptively on high alert so that danger can be avoided and our survival maintained. The naggings of negativity and pessimism, therefore, which we cannot seem to completely shed even with an ever increasing plethora of self-help and positive-thinking books and perhaps even with ongoing counseling and psychotherapy, appear more understandable or even "normal" when we take into account the vast history of human experience accumulated and recorded in the brain. Our brain is continually evaluating both the external and internal environments for any and all signs of risk or danger through the process of *neuroception,* a term that has been coined by the neuroscientist Stephen Porges. "Because of our heritage as a species," writes Porges, "neuroception takes place in primitive parts of the brain, without our conscious awareness" (2011, p. 11). Each of us, in other words, by way of the negativity or vigilance bias of the brain is predisposed to be somewhat anxious and on alert for any threat or danger that potentially may come from either the external environment and/or our own internal world. It therefore reflects "a past-biased assessment of safety and danger" (Siegel, 2010, p. 21), largely based on our collective experience and history as a human race as well as our own individual histories. Even though we are not always aware of it on a conscious or cognitive level, "our body has already started a sequence of neural processes that would facilitate adaptive defense behaviors such as fight, flight, or freeze" (Porges, 2011, p. 11).

While this is not a book on brain anatomy, it is necessary to have at least a basic understanding of certain areas of the brain that are central to defensive fight-flight-freeze patterns of emotion and behavior. As Siegel argues in *The Mindful Therapist,* having a basic knowledge "about brain function and structure is empowering for people—and having terms that are not intimidating and relate to everyday life can be extremely useful" (2010, p. 139). Moreover, I would argue that it in an age of heightened anxiety and uncertainty, pastoral and spiritual caregivers as well as pastoral counselors and psychotherapists must develop enough of a working knowledge of brain function and structure to consistently make informed and effective interventions with anxious congregants and clients. There is at present some controversy about the use of the term "limbic system" to refer to the "emotional brain" or the center of human emotion in contrast to human cognition. In previous decades, research linked specific brain areas to emotional responses, "many involving subcortical or old cortical regions, as opposed to neocortex, a trend that led to the view that the brain does indeed have a special emotion system" (LeDoux, 2002, p. 201). Cognition, by and large, was assumed to reside in the more recently evolved and higher-order neocortex region of the brain, while human emotion was located in the older and more primitive regions of limbic activity. It has now been demonstrated that the brain is far too complex to relegate cognition here and emotion there, as if there can be a separate and distinct emotional center of the brain. Cognitive function and emotional activity continuously rely on overlapping regions of the brain, perhaps illustrating quintessentially that human beings, in the words of the psalmist, are indeed fearfully and wonderfully made (Psalm

139:14). That said, there is some practical value in retaining the limbic system as a conceptual framework, particularly for the purposes of educating pastoral and spiritual caregivers about certain basic brain functions. Joseph LeDoux, one of the foremost critics of the limbic system theory, while ultimately abandoning the concept has still noted that the original ideas supporting it

> are insightful and quite interesting in the context of a general evolutionary explanation of emotion and the brain. In particular, the notion that emotions involve relatively primitive circuits that are conserved throughout mammalian evolution seems right on target (2002, p. 212).

The limbic system of the brain is comprised of several structures that directly support and reinforce the naggings of pessimism and a vigilant predisposition. The oldest structure in the human limbic system, referred to by Andrew Newberg as the "master controller," is the hypothalamus, which "can help create basic emotions such as rage and terror as well as positive states ranging from moderate pleasure to bliss" (2002, pp. 43–44). A sort of "thermostat" for the body, it helps to regulate the intensity of our emotional and visceral responses in order to maintain a state of homeostasis. Next in the limbic system is the structure that is central to and particularly relevant for the study of neuroplasticity in the context of pastoral and spiritual care, what Newberg refers to as the "ancient limbic watchdog" (2002, p. 67): the amygdala, an almond-shaped cluster of neurons in the brain. The principle function of the amygdala is that of surveillance and vigilance, always on guard and on alert for any and all signs of potential threat and danger. I will have more to say about this neural watchdog, the alarm and warning center of the brain, shortly. Lastly, there is what Newberg calls the limbic "diplomat," the hippocampus that unlike the amygdala and hypothalamus "does not directly generate emotion, but by its regulatory effects upon other key parts of the brain, it exerts great influence upon an individual's state of mind" (2002, p. 46). The hippocampus performs its regulatory function by weaving together "the basic forms of emotional and perceptual memory into factual and autobiographical recollections" (Siegel, 2011, p. 19). These are the neural clusters of memory that we discussed in the previous chapter, which for better and in certain cases for worse are reactivated all the time and therefore bias the way we perceive and interact with the world and other human beings around us. All the time, in your brain and mine, the amygdala is scanning the external environment as well as the internal world of thoughts, feelings, and sensations to detect any signs of threat and danger and consequently to trigger a fear response if necessary: a frown from the boss, the argument with a spouse, a drop in the stock market, a body ache or pain, prayers to God going unanswered, what does it all mean? Rapidly, the mind scours familiar memory banks of information, sorting and cross-referencing vast quantities of data until it can resolve the confusion or the problem at hand. "The computational task," writes Newberg, "is staggering, but in an instant, all the brain's memory files have been consulted, all irrelevant data has been ignored...uncertainty causes anxiety, and anxiety must be resolved" (2002, pp. 67 & 70).

It is worth taking a closer look at the amygdala in order to gain a more in-depth understanding of the brain's bias and predisposition toward negativity and why it can be challenging, to say the least, to follow more consistently the teaching of Jesus on anxiety. For millennia, the amygdala has guided the human race to safety and survival through, in the words of the hymn, many dangers, toils, and snares, and it remains primed and ready to keep us safe in the future. In a sense, we owe it a debt of gratitude, for you and I and everyone else would not be here today without it. The perils of an ice age, incessant wars, the collapse of empires and civilizations, deadly plagues and epidemics, and countless other recorded and unrecorded events when human survival hung in the balance required no shortage of vigilance, which the brain has never forgotten. To be sure, the presence of a hypervigilant survival mechanism in the brain that prompts us to preemptively avoid painful situations first and ask questions later is the reason we are all here today. Human beings, in ages past on the Serengeti, would not have survived if they had repeatedly assumed that up ahead is probably nothing to worry about, no doubt just a patch of dead grass and nothing more. Historically and evolutionarily, it has often been in our best interests to assume the worst, to follow the prompting of the amygdala and assume that the light-brownish shape up ahead *is* something more than dead grass, perhaps a lion. "So the visual stimulus goes straight to the amygdala; only later does it work its way up through the visual cortex for processing and analysis" (McEwen, 2002, p. 37).

The same can be said for myriad stimuli that we receive today, including but not limited to the visual: the visual stimulus of the boss' frown, the auditory stimulus of a spouse's voiced frustration, and/or the tactile stimulus of something that feels unusual or suspicious after performing a self-examination of one's body, it all goes straight to the amygdala in a split second and only later does it make its way up through the sensory cortex for more in-depth processing and analysis. In an instant, the amygdala has activated all the brain's memory files in an urgent attempt to make sense of the present situation, for as we have learned uncertainty causes anxiety and for the amygdala anxiety must be dealt with and resolved immediately. "Amygdala activation, in other words, turns a plain perceptual experience into a fearful one" (LeDoux, 2002, p. 225). It can also, as Gazzaniga describes with a practical example familiar to all of us, take a relatively minor negative occurrence and exaggerate the situation disproportionately, even to the point of ruining an evening out at dinner:

> The amygdala not only affects your motor system but can also change your thinking. Your quick emotional response of fear or disgust or anger to the threatening (negative) incoming information will color how you process further information. It concentrates your attention on the negative stimulus. You are not thinking the mozzarella looks fresh, the basil is fragrant, the tomatoes are red and juicy; you are thinking, *Yuck, there is a greasy hair on my plate, and I am not going to eat this. In fact, I am never eating here again.* This is our negativity bias (2008, p. 123).

This bias or predisposition to turn ordinary situations and perceptual experiences into more than they often are, to pessimistically assume the worst and to worry again and again about tomorrow is not a sign of personal failure or moral weakness, or to use the theological term, sin, unless by the latter we are in agreement with Paul Tillich that "sin is a universal fact before it becomes an individual act" (1975, p. 56). Rather, the negativity and vigilance bias of the brain simply reflects the human condition at the present moment, the present state of our collective development. This is a paradigmatic reframe of sin to be sure, as we align it more closely with the neuroscientific perspective of LeDoux expressed in the previous chapter: the limited state of human development and experience at present simply reflects that certain newly evolved neural structures are not as fully integrated into the brain. I will have more to say about the theological reframing of sin, specifically the reframing of original sin, in the next chapter. For now, it is worth noting that the cerebral cortex, which includes the prefrontal cortex, appears higher up in the brain above the limbic system, indicating that it is the most recent structure to appear in the history of brain evolution. The human brain has evolved from the bottom up as it were, along what neuroscientists call the *neuroaxis*, so that the limbic system sits atop the brainstem and the cerebral cortex atop the limbic region. Within the cortex, the prefrontal network is thought to perform executive or higher-order functions related to more complex thinking and problem solving, self-regulation, impulse control, and social behavior. From this we can conclude that

> The lower levels have more direct control over the body and less capacity to change their own neural networks. The upper levels are the opposite: although they are more removed from the action, they have greater neuroplasticity—the capacity to be shaped by neural/mental activity, to learn from experience. At all levels of the neuroaxis, the intentions—the goals and related strategies—at work operate mainly outside of our awareness....In general, the farther down the neuroaxis a response takes place, the faster, more intense, and more automatic it is. Higher on the neuroaxis, responses become more delayed, less intense, and more considered. In particular, the cortex—the most evolutionari-

ly recent level—really enhances our capacity to take the future into account. Usually, the longer the view, the wiser the intentions (Hanson, 2009, pp. 100 & 107).

As we learned in the previous chapter, optimistic messages of love, hope, and reassurance that emerge from the higher levels on the neuroaxis can and certainly do influence us and our outlook on life for the better, just not with the same galvanic and visceral effect as the messages coming from further down in the limbic region. Thus, the older the neural structure and further down the neuroaxis it goes, the more direct control and influence it will exert on body, mind, and memory. The amygdala, for example, a very old structure indeed in the history of brain evolution, works to keep us on guard and watchful every single moment of the day. Anxious and vigilant awareness has kept our prehistoric and historic ancestors alive in the face of grave dangers and grim circumstances, and as far as the amygdala is concerned the same degree of hypervigilance will continue to support human survival in the present and the future. The only difficulty, as Seligman noted earlier, is that the deep and pervasive naggings of pessimism and vigilant awareness are increasingly excessive for and incommensurate with life in the postmodern world. Still, the vestiges of the ice-age brain, the Black-Death brain, and so on linger in the collective memory bank, to the extent that emotional arousal in the brain continues to powerfully influence the processing of the higher levels of executive function. "Attention, perception, memory, decision-making, and the conscious concomitants of each are all swayed in emotional states" (LeDoux, 2002, p. 225), particularly those anxious and fearful states generated by the amygdala. LeDoux refers to this neural conversion process as "the hostile takeover of consciousness by emotion" (2002, p. 226), with the amygdala initiating an alteration of consciousness from higher-order thinking and reflection to a more primitive state of fearful emotion at any given moment. How, exactly, does the amygdala achieve this split-second alteration, triggering an instant downshifting in the higher order functions of the brain in deference to the more primal circuits invested in our immediate preservation and survival? For LeDoux, "emotion comes to monopolize consciousness, at least in the domain of fear, when the amygdala comes to dominate working memory" (2002, p. 226).

It should be clear by now that the amygdala, the almond-shaped neural structure of the limbic region, functions as the alarm system or early-warning center in the brain, detecting any and all threats and dangers to our survival, happiness, and well-being. As such, it "is hardwired to focus on negative information and react intensely to it" (2009, p. 53), entirely invested in alerting us to and preempting any real and potential pain, suffering, and unhappiness. An anticipatory neural structure par excellence, the amygdala is forever prompting our vigilant awareness by sounding the alarm, whether there is anything to legitimately worry about or not. Even something as ordinary as anticipating an upcoming challenging event, such as giving a talk or presentation in the next week, "can have as much impact as living through it for real" (Hanson, 2009, p. 52). The amygdala sounds the alarm bell ahead of time, anticipatorily: What will I say? Will it go well? Will the audience like it? Will they think I know what I am talking about, or not? Imagine if the particular threat or danger is more immediate and real and ominous to an individual with a history of trauma, neglect, and/or abuse, and how the amygdala will fire up with even greater force and intensity. Consciousness and higher-order neural functions, as LeDoux has demonstrated, are taken over and monopolized by emotion, as the amygdala comes to dominate the working memory of any given moment. In fact, "when the amygdala detects a threat, it triggers consequences that ultimately place working memory in a vigilant processing state, causing it to continue to attend to whatever it is occupied with at the moment, biasing thoughts, decisions, and actions" (LeDoux, 2002, p. 289). Put another way, the amygdala, in the face of a real or potential threat or danger, will in a sense hijack and hold captive the higher-order executive functions of the brain and dominate the working-memory interpretation of the given moment.

From Siegel's research, we learned that neurons that fire together wire together, so that our experience, whether negative or positive or simply neutral, becomes encoded and interpreted by myriad neural clusters of memory. If we experience an internal event, such as a painful thought or feeling, or an external event that we perceive to be threatening in any way, the amygdala will alter consciousness by reactivating, sometimes disproportionately, anxious and fearful memory patterns. Again, we would not be here today if it were not for the negativity bias of the brain, in particular that of the amygdala structure, nor would we even be able to engage in everyday life without its innate guidance. The amygdala, as LeDoux points out, has simplified life for all of us by applying previous learning, individually and collectively, to present experience. For example, its synapses are wired by nature to respond to a lion on the Serengeti, "and by experience to respond in the same way to dangers that are learned about" (LeDoux, 2002, p. 7). LeDoux goes on to say, with words that in certain ways parallel those of the psalmist, that "it is a wonderfully efficient way to do things":

> Rather than create a separate system to accommodate learning about new dangers, just enable the system that is already evolutionarily wired to detect danger to be modifiable by experience. The brain can, as a result, deal with novel dangers by taking advantage of evolutionarily fine-tuned ways of responding. All it has to do is create a synaptic substitution whereby the new stimulus can enter the circuits that the prewired ones used....The basic wiring plan is simple: it involves the synaptic delivery of information about the outside world to the amygdala, and the control of responses that act back on the

world by synaptic outputs of the amygdala. If the amygdala detects something dangerous via its inputs, then its outputs are engaged. The result is freezing, changes in blood pressure and heart rate, release of hormones, and lots of other responses that either are programmed ways of dealing with danger or are aspects of body physiology that support defensive behaviors. ...Most systems of the brain are plastic, that is, modifiable by experience, which means that the synapses involved are changed by experience. But, as the fear example shows, learning is not the function that those systems were originally designed to perform. They were built instead to accomplish certain tasks (like detecting danger, finding food and mates, hearing sounds, or moving a limb toward some desired object). Learning (synaptic plasticity) is just a feature that helps them do their job better (2002, pp. 7–9).

A SURPLUS OF NEGATIVITY AND VIGILANCE

The vestiges of negativity and pessimism run deep in the human brain and nervous system, the residual buildup of vast stretches of human prehistory and history. Put another way, we all bear the accumulated activity and experience of countless generations of human beings, which, perhaps somewhat akin to tree rings, is recorded and stored away in each of our brains for future reference and reactivation. The amygdala, armed with this vast storehouse of information and experience, is forever scanning the external environment and the inner world for any immediate and/or potential threat or danger, priming us to be on guard and ready to respond. "Occasionally," notes Hanson, "this vigilance is warranted, but usually it is excessive, driven by amygdala-hippocampus reactions to past events that are no longer likely" (2009, p. 88). And the operative word in today's world is *occasionally*, revealing that while at certain times vigilance is of course warranted and necessary in cases of immediate threat and danger, more often than not it is disproportionate to the situation. Military personnel, for example, who are in harm's way need a vigilant and in certain cases a hypervigilant awareness while engaged in combat in order to stay alive. The same with those who have witnessed violence in their communities and therefore feel a need to be on high alert as individuals and as a neighborhood. And for the individual who has witnessed and/or been the victim of abuse and domestic violence in his or her own home, a high level of vigilance and amygdala-hippocampus reactivity is understandable and to be expected. That said, even for those who carry the effects of post-traumatic stress and vigilance prompted by the neural memory clusters of painful events and experiences in the past, there comes a time to begin recognizing, often in psychotherapy and pastoral counseling, the disproportionate negativity and vigilance being attributed to benign experiences in the present. But even for those of us who have never faced mortal combat or witnessed drive-by shootings or been the victim of domestic abuse and violence, we too have experienced at one time or another painful and difficult circumstances, traumatic losses, personal and relational crises, and so forth. Thus, all of us are driven, to one extent or another, by amygdala-hippocampus reactions to past events in our personal lives as well as to myriad events in the prehistory and history of the human race. This excessive negativity and vigilance, as the therapist or pastoral counselor would say to clients in his or her care, is completely understandable given their personal histories on top of human history, and yet so often it is not desirable in the context of their *present* lives. Moreover, the stress that results from vigilant awareness that is excessive and disproportionate "is unnecessary and unpleasant, and it primes the brain and body to overreact to small things" (Hanson, 2009, p. 88).

Each of us today is the bearer of a residual level of vigilance that fit the situation well vis-à-vis the dangers of the Serengeti, the grim realities of an ice age, unrelenting wars and deadly plagues, and so on. Added to these neural clusters of inherited memory are those we have accumulated along the way of our personal lives, which reinforce our brain's hardwired predisposition to be even more watchful and vigilant. This feeling to be alert at all times, as we have learned, evolved to protect us in environments that were much more dangerous than anything most of us face today. It is why the brain is still today like Velcro for negativity and like Teflon for positivity, why negativity resonates with more visceral force and energy even if we fill our hearts and minds with the wisdom amassed from self-help and positive-thinking resources. Neurologically, we come hardwired with a surplus of negativity and vigilance that is often excessive and disproportionate in everyday life, particularly in the context of our relationships. Whether the relationship be marital, parental, vocational, a friendship, and/or any combination of these, we are predisposed to be on the lookout for any sign of threat that might be indicative of, respectively, our spouse or partner falling out of love with us, our child not growing up to be a responsible person, the boss thinking of terminating our employment, a trusted friend no longer being reliable. Additionally, the excessive vigilance can be within ourselves, as the so-called inner judge or critic never ceases to remind us how often we have fallen short in our marriage, at work, as a parent or friend, in our spiritual life with God, and what the potential consequences might be for us going forward. As Barbara Fredrickson has observed in her important research on positivity, "people typically experience positive and negative emotional states at different intensities and frequencies"; negativity is experienced more intensely in the brain, as we have already learned, and this creates an "asymmetry" that can surely be construed as a "negativity bias" (2009, p. 144). The built-in negativity bias of the brain has been a godsend in terms of human survival strategies, but the surplus that we and those in our care have inherited now leads to so much unnecessary suffering. As Hanson observes, the human brain in its present shape and form "is fertile ground for a harvest of suffering." He adds:

Only we humans worry about the future, regret the past, and blame ourselves for the present. We get frustrated when we cannot have what we want, and disappointed when what we like ends. We suffer *that* we suffer. We get upset about being in pain, angry about dying, sad about waking up sad yet another day. This kind of suffering—which encompasses most of our unhappiness and dissatisfaction—is constructed by the brain. It is made up. Which is ironic, poignant—and supremely hopeful. For if the brain is the cause of suffering, it can also be its cure (2009, p. 12).

We will discuss in detail the flip side of the equation, the brain's capacity to heal and rewire itself more in the direction of peace and joy and positivity, when we focus on contemplative-meditational practices and mindfulness- and acceptance-based therapeutic strategies in later chapters. For now, it is important to keep in mind that even when we are deeply committed to a spiritual life of growth and healing and change, the asymmetrical negativity bias is still operative and always will be operative in our brain. Fredrickson has even quantified the neurological asymmetry, demonstrating with her re-search that at the present moment of our collective human development it is clearly not an even match between negativity and positivity in the brain. The data she has collected lead her to conclude that in order for us to achieve and maintain a basic level of neural balance and equilibrium, there must be at least a three-to-one ratio of positivity to negativity. We have already learned that what makes a marriage work, among other things, is an even higher ratio of five positives to one negative. After years of relationship and marriage analysis, John Gottman, as we briefly noted in the previous chapter, has discovered that for every negative interaction experienced by a couple (an argument or disagreement, a critical word or condescending look, forgetting an important date or occasion, and so forth), there must be at least five positive affirmations and interactions to keep the relationship or marriage in balance. Gottman, even after a single session with couples, can now after decades of empirical and longitudinal research predict with more than ninety-percent accuracy those couples that are destined to grow and thrive and stay together and those that will not. By looking for the predictors of divorce, the telltale warning signs that he refers to as the "four horsemen of the apoca-lypse," Gottman emphasizes that he is accurately "able to predict whether a couple will stay happily together or lose their way," and that he can make this prediction after listening to the couple communicate and interact "for as little as five minutes" (1999, p. 2). And the specific "horsemen" that he is looking for when meeting with a couple, whether they are manifested directly or more often indirectly and subtly by the spouses or partners, are criticism, contempt, defensiveness, and stonewalling. In the context of marital life, each time a marriage partner is critical of the other, each time a spouse defensively refuses to talk about an issue of importance or urgency to the other, there will need to be five positive acts of love and affirmation for the couple to maintain its relational balance.

Gottman's extensive research on marriage is clearly indicative of the negativity bias of the brain, that at the present moment of human brain evolution we feel and experience negativity with far more galvanic force and energy than we do positivity, particularly with those closest to us that we love the most. The surplus of negativity and vigilance spills over all the time in our marriages and in our closest relationships, no matter how mindful and spiritually centered we try to be. Siegel, an expert in the science of mindfulness, has already recounted for us the rather humbling experience of letting his negativity get the better of him as a parent, with the "crepes of wrath" story. The surplus of negativity and vigilance, to be sure, extends beyond marriage into every dimension of human life and in particular every dimension of human relational life. From Fredrickson's more extensive research, we are now able to quantify that in general it takes a three-to-one ratio of positivity to negativity for human individuals to more fully grow and develop in their lives. If our ratio of positivity to negativity is at least three-to-one, we have a much better chance of experiencing what Fredrickson calls "human flourishing," perhaps somewhat akin to the "abundant life" put forward by Jesus. The finding in fact now serves as a "tipping point" in the study of human development and well-being, leading to the "bold prediction that only when positivity ratios are higher than three-to-one is positivity in sufficient supply to seed human flourishing" (Fredrickson, 2009, p. 129). For Fredrickson, while the neural deck is stacked against us clearly in favor of a negative predisposition, we are not entirely at the mercy of the current of our thoughts and emotions. Rather, the promise of neuroplasticity means that we can begin to alter the course of its flow, to move the "riverbed" of our thinking and our emotionality to an increasingly higher baseline level. "No matter where your river of emotions flows today," she writes, "over time and with continued effort and attention, we can change its course and location" (Fredrickson, 2009, p. 155). This careful and continued focus of attention, as we have learned, slows down activity in the limbic area of the brain, particularly the fearful and vigilant activity of the amygdala structure, while simultaneously increasing the higher-order processing in the prefrontal cortex. Moreover, harnessing the power of our attention and awareness, as Siegel has demonstrated, amplifies neuroplasticity in the brain by enhancing the structural growth of synaptic linkages among the activated neurons.

Still, it is important for pastoral and spiritual caregivers not to, on the one hand, minimize in these anxious and uncertain times the powerful predisposition toward negativity and vigilance hardwired into the brain. On the other hand, as we will see in the next chapter, we must guard against applying even inadvertently religious beliefs and theological views that unnecessarily strengthen and reinforce the ingrained negativity bias of those in our care.

Ultimately, the goal of our pastoral or spiritual care is to help congregants and clients *reduce* their level of negativity and anxious awareness rather than, as they might have hoped, eliminate it once and for all. Sometimes negative emotions, such as grief that helps us process the loss of a loved one and anger that helps us become more constructively engaged in fighting injustice and inequality, keep us emotionally honest and spiritually grounded. This is what Fredrickson describes as "appropriate negativity," which she distinguishes from a "gratuitous negativity" that is more excessive and disproportionate to any given situation. She comments that "whereas some of our negativity is corrective and energizing, not all of it is....gratuitous negativity is neither helpful nor healthy" (2009, p. 159). Recalling that neurons that fire together will wire together with even greater force and intensity, we can surmise that if we let our negative thoughts and emotions go on unchecked about past or present events and circumstances, about ourselves and other people that we know or perhaps do not even know, we diminish our potential to flourish and to live abundantly. The gratuitous grumblings of negativity add up over time, so that "while the movie is running, our neurons are wiring together" (Hanson, 2009, p. 162). It is therefore not the elimination of negativity that we work toward in our pastoral or clinical practice, but rather a reduction in its gratuitous manifestations. With the practicalities of life in mind, Fredrickson asks us rhetorically,

> Does it help to snap at the cashier after you have waited in line longer than you expected? Is it healthy to berate yourself for not getting the laundry done? What is to be gained when you dwell on an off-the-cuff comment a co-worker made? At times your entrenched emotional habits can intensify or prolong your bad feelings far beyond their usefulness. Your negativity becomes corrosive and smothering. Like an out-of-control weed, gratuitous negativity grows fast and crowds out positivity's more tender shoots (2009, p. 159).

Chapter Three

The Impact of Theology on the Brain

The kingdom of God cometh not with observation: Neither shall they say, Lo here! or, lo there! for, behold, the kingdom of God is within you.—Jesus, Luke 17:20–21 (KJV)

It is striking that in another teaching, this time on the kingdom of God and heaven, Jesus locates the kingdom not in some celestial corner of the universe or at a distant point in the future but rather in the present lived experience of the human person. There are and always will be those who state grandiosely that the kingdom is externally located here or over there or is coming any day now, dramatically if not apocalyptically, with clouds descending. Yet, according to Jesus, the kingdom is not an external phenomenon that can be observed with the human sensory system, for it is more fundamental to human life and experience and to our very being. As the spiritual teacher Eckhart Tolle has noted, commenting on various teachings from the ancient world, the precise meaning of the kingdom of God or heaven connotes the simple but profound peace and joy of being (2005, p. 43). In many ways it parallels what Jesus was conveying in what some believe to be the core message of his gospel: "I have come that they may have life, and that they may have it more abundantly" (John 10:10). The kingdom of abundance and joy is in you and me, and thus is a reflection of our inherent value and goodness. It is like treasure hidden in a field, waiting to be discovered, a pearl of inestimable worth. If as Jesus teaches the kingdom is more immediate and less remote, located in the profound joy of human being, then you and I and all human beings are the manifestation of this treasure. We do not look for it here or over there, or wait for it to come to us, for the treasure of the kingdom is already in us, woven into the fabric of our very being.

A NECESSARY AND TIMELY SHIFT IN PARADIGMS

The core of Jesus' parabolic teaching is reminiscent of the wisdom of Eastern philosophy and spirituality, that most fundamentally human beings share an original goodness and worth, a hidden treasure as it were. But the treasure at times, at least in Judeo-Christian circles, has been hidden by layer upon layer of theologizing about our innate sinfulness. Theologians down through the centuries have given an initial and oftentimes superficial nod to the fact that we are created Imago Dei and therefore originally good, only to launch into more substantive efforts intended to demonstrate what has become a more compelling narrative: the theology of original sin. A sense of wrongfulness, the feeling that something is fundamentally not right with us, is nothing new of course, as Donald Capps articulated in his book, *The Depleted Self*. Capps noted that historically in the Western world this way of viewing human nature and existence has been based on a theology and a psychology of guilt. The combined force of classical Judeo-Christian theology, where we stand in need of undeserved forgiveness for our debts and trespasses, and that of psychoanalysis, where we are expected to come to terms with the original guilt from early oedipal experience, reinforces the sense of wrongfulness stemming from an original guilt. What is new, in Capps' estimation, is the way we experience our sense of innate wrongfulness:

> In our times, we are much more likely to experience this "wrongfulness" according to shame, rather than guilt, dynamics. Thus, to speak meaningfully and relevantly about sin, we have to relate sin to the experience of shame—not only, not even primarily, to the experience of guilt. Obviously, this will involve a reformulation of our theology of sin, a reformulation that is so deep and extensive that it calls for a fundamental change in our theological paradigm (1993, p. 3).

[handwritten margin note: we are more likely to believe we are bad than we did a bad thing]

Building on Capps' paradigmatic shift, I too am arguing for a fundamental change in the prevailing theological paradigm, only now with neuroscientific findings in hand I intend to take the discussion even further. Capps' research demonstrated rather clearly that based on the actual experience of those living in an age of narcissism, a theology of original sin rooted in the dynamics of guilt increasingly had less resonance. Instead, a theology of wrongfulness based more on the prevailing dynamics of shame would, Capps argued, resonate more clearly and forcefully for individuals living in a narcissistic age. At the time I completely agreed with this important paradigm shift, and still do relative to that period of time in the 1990s. But now we find ourselves living in another age that is characterized by a constant and pervasive anxiety about the present and future state of the nation, the world, the planet, and so on. Simultaneous with this pronounced spike in anxiety is a growing interest in neuroscientific research, which as we have already seen has demonstrated rather clearly that the human brain has a remarkable capacity to change itself throughout the entire lifespan. By training the mind to rewire the brain, largely through the spiritual practices of contemplative prayer and mindfulness meditation, we can position ourselves to live more abundantly and more simply in the profound peace and joy of being.

That said, it is equally important for pastoral and spiritual caregivers to keep in mind that the treasure of abundant life, so central to Jesus' gospel message, can at times be difficult to locate let alone embrace with any sense of joy. We have already seen that the brain comes with a built-in "negativity bias," so often originating in amygdala-driven activity and reactivity to even the slightest hint of threat. And although it is true that we would not be here today if it were not for the deeply ingrained impulse to look for any sign of negativity all around us, in today's world the level of alertness and vigilance is often disproportionate if not excessive. Rather than constantly scanning the external world for all kinds of threats and dangers, the surplus of anxious and negative awareness is redirected inward on ourselves and toward our very own human nature. One of the principle ways to turn the tables on ourselves, theologically and psychologically, is to cling to paradigmatic frameworks that fundamentally run counter to the peace and joy of being and to abundant life. In the 1990s, Donald Capps rightly encouraged a necessary paradigm shift away from a theology of original sinfulness based on the dynamics of guilt to one based more relevantly on the dynamics of shame. What I am suggesting is that in an age increasingly informed by the findings of neuroscience, most notably that the brain is built for change through the process of neuroplasticity, we have reached a time when it is necessary to further reassess any and all theological and psychological constructs in terms of their capacity to enhance and/or thwart the process of growth and change. This will represent a more extensive paradigm shift for pastoral and spiritual care, one that, building on the work of Capps, takes fully into account the present-day lived experience of the human person. A theological construct of original sin and inherent wrongfulness, however we decide to slice it in today's world, will reinforce to one extent or another the negativity bias of the brain, which then becomes an impediment to fully experiencing the fundamental joy of abundant life.

What we learned in the previous chapter is that the human brain, at this stage of our collective development, focuses more on negative information than on positive experiences and thus considerably more attention and energy is directed toward what is potentially wrong and problematic in our lives. Negative experiences, real and/or imagined, stick to our brains like Velcro while more positive and joyful experiences tend to roll off the brain as if it were Teflon. Even though our day-to-day experiences are often neutral and in certain cases quite positive, the brain will most certainly recall any negativity with more galvanic and visceral force. The higher cortical regions of the brain, as we have seen, are a more recent development than the more primitive areas of limbic activity. Within the latter is lodged the powerful alert or warning center that is the amygdala, the part of the brain that is ever scanning the horizon for the slightest hint of threat or danger. Historically, the dangers were always external to the human person, over the next hill or ridge or around the next bend on the Serengeti. More recently, however, as human civilization has evolved beyond a constant level of danger toward a more relative state of stability, the focus increasingly has become internal. Copious amounts of time and energy and money have been spent looking for what is wrong with us, medically and psychologically. The latest edition of the *Diagnostic and Statistical Manual of Mental Disorders*, the *DSM-V*, reveals that diagnoses of what is wrong with us continue to grow exponentially and no doubt to the satisfaction of pharmaceutical conglomerates. The negativity bias of the brain is therefore reinforced by the bio-medically constructed model of psychiatry and counseling, which encourages therapists to be on the lookout for any and all signs of psychological maladies and mental disorders. While there is a growing trend among clinical practitioners to give as much and in some cases more attention to mental wellness as to mental illness, it will be some time before the two poles are on equal footing. Human beings, even those of us who are educated and clinically trained, are inherently biased toward the negative, sometimes more than we realize. And the bias becomes reinforced by a certain psychological constructivism that we assume is consistently based on empirical data and evidence. Ironically, psychiatry's preoccupation with mental illness reflects and further reinforces the ingrained negativity bias of the brain, keeping us trapped in familiar ways of thinking, knowing, diagnosing, and treating.

The same, I would argue, can be said of theological constructivism, specifically, the *construct* of original sin, which conveys that human beings post-creation are innately flawed and in need of spiritual repair. Theology's historical focus on the internal dangers of original sin and human depravity similarly reflects and reinforces deeply ingrained neural pathways of negativity in the brain. We can see this without any difficulty in John Calvin's theological anthropology, which is readily apparent from the outset of the *Institutes*. Lurking within the human person, according to Calvin, is "a veritable world of miseries" and "a teeming horde of infamies" (1960, p. 36). While I find Calvin's Reformed theology valuable and even foundational for my own work of pastoral care and counseling, particularly the way he connects knowledge of God with knowledge of self and vice versa, it must be noted that he like anyone else has been guided to some extent by a negativity bias, in this case twofold: neurological and theological. To know God, according to Calvin, presupposes that I have a thoroughgoing knowledge of myself, which I find quite helpful. But, and herein lies the rub, how is this even possible if from the outset of my theological reflection I am biased to see myself and others fundamentally as a world of miseries and a horde of infamies? While I personally need little reminder of my own limitations and imperfections, and certainly not one so fatalistic, the more fundamental issue in light of neuroscientific research, specifically that of Darbara Fredrickson, is how I and other pastoral and spiritual practitioners make use of theology and spiritual practices to increase the ratio of positivity to negativity and not the other way around.

The importance of grounding ourselves, personally and professionally, not so much in the awareness of any original wrongdoing but more in the positivity of our present lived experience, is clearly supported by the findings of neuroscience. As we intentionally use the mind to rewire the brain, thus fostering the process of neuroplasticity, we discover that the neurally in-grained predisposition to anxiously look for any hint of threat or danger outside *and* within ourselves can over time be more neutralized. Through a daily practice of contemplative prayer and mindfulness meditation, we can begin to train our mind and brain to focus more on the inherent joy of life and the blessing of God's abiding love and presence, and less on what is wrong with life and with us. This does not always come so easily, at least not initially, for we are in fact going against the grain of ancient currents deeply lodged in the central nervous system and against a powerful evolutionary template. The negativity bias, at least at the present moment of human histo-ry and development, has tremendous power over the way we view our lives, ourselves, our relationships, and the world. In other words, the "bad stuff," as Bruce McEwan puts it, still has priority and will continue to have priority for some time to come. Positive messages of love, kindness, and compassion are not lost on the human brain and body and do in fact have a discernible influence, but ultimately they have less resonance and effect than do negative messages and constructs. McEwen adds that

> It is telling that more neural pathways go from the fear and emotional centers to the "higher up" regions, like the cortex, than come back down from the lofty heights into the stress response's engine room....As [we] navigate the perils of evolution, the positive emotions tend to take a backseat (2002, pp. 148–149).

THE NEUROLOGICAL IMPACT OF THE ADAMIC MYTH

If we apply the findings of neuroscience to Judeo-Christian theology, we will see that it is not at all surprising that the construct of original sin has been so foundational to religious thought and practice. We are, after all, neurological-ly predisposed to focus more on the negativity of life than on the joy and goodness of God's creation. In the Western world, there is a deep resonance with the message that something is fundamentally wrong with us, that some-how restitution must be made for an original wrongful action on the part of humanity back in the distant past and, additionally, that we must somehow hope for a more joyful scenario in the world to come. The theological view that there is something fundamentally wrong with us or more precisely that we are originally sinful, when viewed from the standpoint of neuroscience, is a considerable obstacle to experiencing life in all its fullness. With the promise of neuroplasticity in mind, Andrew Newberg argues that it is imperative for religions to "allow for some degree of adaptability so that they can maintain their relevance in a changing world" (2010, p. 109). To maintain a certain relevance and vitality in the age of neuroscience will require from pastoral and spiritual practitioners the reframing of theological views that reinforce the brain's predisposition toward negativity and anxious awareness. Recalling the words of Tara Brach from chapter one, the more we acknowledge and reinforce the meta-narrative about what is wrong with us and/or with others, the more we deepen the neural pathways that generate and amplify feelings of deficiency. In Judeo-Christian theological terms, to overlook or worse to dismiss the findings of neuroplasticity and instead cling to a theology of original sin and innate wrongfulness will simply reinforce the neural grooves and pathways that keep us from fully experiencing the peace and joy of God's presence. Paul Ricoeur, writing in the 1970s and therefore on the edge of the early emergence of modern neuroscience, had already issued a resounding critique of the familiar theological view that sees a need to make restitution in the present for what has reportedly been done in the distant past:

> We are here at the source of the schema of *inheritance* which we have found at the basis of the Adamic speculation from Saint Paul to Saint Augustine…it will never be said just what evil has been done to Christianity by the literal interpretation, the historicist interpretation, of the Adamic myth. This interpretation has plunged Christianity into the profession of an absurd history and into pseudo-rational speculations on the quasi-biological transmission of a quasi-juridical guilt for the fault of an *other* man, back into the night of time, somewhere between Pithecanthropus and Neanderthal man (2004, p. 280).

It is also worth returning for a moment to Tillich's methodology for pastoral theology and practice. Earlier we noted that Tillich, if he were living today, would still be making use of the immense and profound material of contemporary scientific and cultural analysis, as he had done so many times before. In this case, the findings of neuroscience would shed new light on the practice of pastoral and spiritual care, and how practitioners would do well to reassess certain theological constructs and their impact on the human mind and brain. It is of particular interest for this study that Tillich, even during the middle part of last century, was already expressing a certain discomfort with the historical interpretation of original sin. Commenting on the doctrine of original sin in *Systematic Theology*, Tillich argued that "reinterpretation is also needed for the terms 'original' and 'hereditary' with respect to sin," and in so doing may at times "demand the rejection of the terms" (1975, p. 46). It is not that the theology of sin, in and of itself, has become obsolete; rather, certain interpretations of it have become problematic when juxtaposed, correlationally, with the findings of neuroscience. For example, the problem for Ricoeur is with the Adamic myth or "Adamic speculation," which traces a continuing thread of original wrongdoing and guilt from the Garden of Eden right up to the present day and age. It has at times been a theological distraction of incalculable proportion, and in the context of pastoral and spiritual care it has undoubtedly been an obstacle to effective practice and therefore to the growth and healing of clients and congregants. The more we focus on original sin, our own and that of those in our care, the less attentional capacity we have for focusing on what is most fundamental to Jesus' gospel: living into the abundance and fullness of human life. Before Ricoeur, however, Tillich had already noted the inherent problems plaguing the doctrine of original and hereditary sin: "Both of these words are so much burdened with literalistic absurdities that it is practically impossible to use them any longer" (1975, p. 46). Later, for Ricoeur, what is most absurd is the schema of inheritance, the historicist interpretation of the Adamic myth, and the pseudo-rational speculations on a biological transmission of spiritual wrongdoing and guilt.

Tillich is not at all arguing for an "I'm OK, you're OK" approach to pastoral theology and practice. Nor does the neuroscientist embrace such a view of human life and existence, given the complexities of the human mind and brain. As Tillich put it so famously, human beings are fundamentally alienated or estranged at some level: from one another, from ourselves or our true self, from God, from life in all its fullness. This, for Tillich, reflects the human condition or universal fact of sin, whereas for the neuroscientist our limited capacity to live more authentically and abundantly and to be less ruled by our fear and anxiety is more a reflection of our present level of collective development. It is surely the price we pay for having only recently evolved higher-order neural capacities, which at some point in the future will become more fully integrated into our brains, just not in our lifetimes. While we will never know the extent to which Tillich would have engaged, correlationally, the data from neuroscientific studies and how it would have informed and been integrated into his theological reflection, we as pastoral and spiritual caregivers can make full use of it to further reassess and reframe the theological construct of *original* sin. Correlationally, from the standpoint of neuroscience, the doctrine does not adequately capture the reality of human finitude and limitation, for this is more a matter of where we are at the present moment of our collective and evolutionary development than anything having to do with any innate sinfulness. Contemporary neuroscience, then, "is giving us new insights into the evolved nature of our species,"

making it directly and immediately relevant to pastoral and spiritual practitioners insofar as we seek, correlationally, "a deeper understanding of what it
means to be human" (Bulkeley, 2005a, p. 219). Any indiscriminate application of the theology of original sin that is not informed by the growing body
of neuroscientific studies and findings will almost certainly have the adverse
effect of triggering the negativity circuitry in the brain. Tillich comments
even further on the immediate need to reassess and reinterpret this complicat-
ed doctrine:

> Theology must join—and in most cases has done so—the historical-critical
> attitude toward the biblical and ecclesiastical myth. Theology further must
> emphasize the positive valuation of man in his essential nature. It must join
> classical humanism in protecting man's created goodness against naturalistic
> and existentialistic denials of his greatness and dignity. At the same time,
> theology should reinterpret the doctrine of original sin by showing man's
> existential self-estrangement and by using the helpful existentialist analyses of
> the human predicament. In doing so, it must develop a realistic doctrine of
> man, in which the ethical and the tragic element in his self-estrangement are
> balanced. It may well be that such a task demands the definite removal from
> the theological vocabulary of terms like "original sin" or "hereditary sin" and
> their replacement by a description of the interpretation of the moral and the
> tragic elements in the human situation (1975, pp. 38–39).

Reflecting on how our constructs, theological and psychological, strengthen
and reinforce the neural connections and synaptic linkages in the brain,
sometimes for the better while in other cases not, Tara Brach also addresses
the Adamic myth that has for millennia been one of the guiding meta-narra-
tives of Western culture. Her commentary on this prevailing cultural myth
and the view of an innate and original sinfulness that goes with it is insight-
ful, coming as it does from someone outside the familiar confines of a Judeo-
Christian theological framework. That she is not a Christian practitioner may
have something to do with her unique insights into the internalization of the
Adamic myth, which is so deeply rooted in the Western mind and brain. The
myth, as Brach notes, has a direct impact on Christian believers and non-
believers alike in the West, even on someone like herself who embraces a
completely different religious and spiritual framework. She links it with the
"trance of unworthiness" that she encounters so often with clients in her
clinical practice. Pastoral and spiritual caregivers see this too, again and
again, with anxious clients and congregants who "embark on one self-improvement project after another," so often "driven by anxious undercurrents
of 'not good enough'" (Brach, 2003, p. 15). While there is something heart-
ening about the dramatic increase in self-help and self-improvement literature in our culture, that more and more people are in fact spiritual seekers,
there is at the same time a shadow side that sometimes gets overlooked. In

our continual quest to become, in the words of TV preacher Joel Osteen (2010), a "better you," we forget that we are riding the never-ending treadmill of self-improvement, that in fact we have become, individually and collectively, a chronic self-improvement project. The neural pathways of negativity that fuel the trance of personal and collective unworthiness run very deep and are further reinforced in the West by certain narratives of our fallen nature and original sinfulness. Ironically, the Adamic myth runs counter to a fundamental trust in our inherent worth and value in the eyes of God, making it particularly challenging, in both mind and brain, to feel more joyful about life and less anxious about tomorrow. Brach observes that

> In stark contrast to trusting in our inherent worth, our culture's guiding myth is the story of Adam and Eve's exile from the Garden of Eden. We may forget its power because it seems so worn and familiar, but this story shapes and reflects the deep psyche of the West. The message of "original sin" is unequivocal: Because of our basically flawed nature, we do not deserve to be happy, loved by others, at ease with life. We are outcasts, and if we are to reenter the garden, we must redeem our sinful selves. We must overcome our flaws by controlling our bodies, controlling our emotions, controlling our natural surroundings, controlling other people. And we must strive tirelessly—working, acquiring, consuming, achieving, e-mailing, overcommitting and rushing—in a never-ending quest to prove ourselves once and for all (2003, p. 12).

After millennia of reinforcement, the Adamic myth of the human fall and our complicit sinfulness has by now carved out a neural pathway of considerable proportion that will require time and patience to rewire. For starters, the rewiring will necessitate an initial shift away from an unexamined confession of original sinfulness toward a daily engagement with contemplative-meditational practices that reflect our inherent worth as people created *Imago Dei*. Over time, our daily spiritual practice will transport us more and more into the joy of and gratitude for our God-given existence. Pastoral and spiritual caregivers would do well to remember that the rewiring of the mind and brain will only take effect through the *regular* practice of contemplative prayer and/or mindfulness meditation, as neuroscience is making clear. "Because our habits of feeling insufficient are so strong, awakening from the trance [of unworthiness]" will involve "not only inner resolve, but also an active training of the heart and mind" (Brach, 2003, p. 3). One of the key findings of neuroscience is that through a *regular* if not *daily* contemplative-meditational practice, we can rewire the neural connections and synaptic linkages in a way that reflects a noticeable rise in our personal positivity to negativity ratio, relative to our overall attitudes and moods.

If the doctrine or theological view of original sin is to have any relevance at all in an age of neuroscience, it will need to be reframed in a way that what we as human beings are confessing is no longer a deep remorse for any innate flaw or defect but rather a mindful and realistic awareness of our collective development at this particular stage of human history. Otherwise, as Donald Capps has demonstrated, there can be a profound disconnect between a core and guiding theological view put forward by pastoral and spiritual caregivers and the present-day lived experience of those in our care. Capps' concern was that Christian theology continued to advance "a perfectly good theory" of human wrongfulness grounded in the dynamics of guilt when in fact the majority of congregants at that time were actually "struggling with the debilitating, demoralizing, and even dehumanizing effects of shame" (1993, p. 35). In short, the concern for theology is to be increasingly mindful of lived experience, lest its core views have diminishing spiritual and psychological resonance. Similarly, to continue maintaining the view of our innate sinfulness in an age of neuroscience, whether it be based on the dynamics of guilt or that of shame, will put Christian theology on a very different wavelength from the growing number of men and women who are increasingly invested in finding ways to live more joyfully and less anxiously in the present moment. This, as I stated at the outset, reflects the correlational view that the great psychological and spiritual challenge of the present day and age is coming to terms with our personal and collective anxiety.

If we and those in our care hope to ground ourselves in the fundamental peace and joy of God's loving presence, we will need to take a thorough inventory of what theological constructs lend support to this endeavor and what constructs are more of an impediment. It should now be clear that the paradigm shift I am suggesting is to move beyond the construct of original sin, at least in the way that it has often been put forward through the centuries. The ascendance of the construct, as Elaine Pagels has argued quite persuasively, completely altered the developmental trajectory of Judeo-Christian theology. While hints of the emerging doctrine can be seen before the third and fourth centuries, it begins to take much deeper root in the Christian psyche following the influential work of St. Augustine, leading to nothing short of a "cataclysmic transformation in Christian thought" (Pagels, 1989, p. 97). We know that in the very early church, more attention was given to the first creation story in Genesis, emphasizing the beauty and grandeur of the created order that was and still is in so many ways very good. However, as Pagels notes, centuries later when the Roman Empire was increasingly threatened by "barbarians at the gates," the theological focus began to shift dramatically away from the splendor of the first creation story in Genesis to the set of unfortunate and tragic circumstances in the second creation story. "Where earlier generations of Jews and Christians had once found in Genesis 1–3 the affirmation of human freedom to choose good or evil, Augustine, living after the age of Constantine, found in the same text a story of human bondage" (Pagels, 1989, p. 97).

As the cognitive therapist would see it, it is mostly a matter of what we choose to focus on, our core beliefs and constructivist views about the world and human life that ultimately shape our view of reality. In this particular case, from Augustine on, Christian theology has invested substantial time and energy focusing on the ontotheology of an inherent human sinfulness, as depicted in the second creation story of Genesis. But what becomes clear through the findings of neuroscience is that such a stark view of original sin has less to do with ultimate reality and more to do with theological constructs that, not surprisingly, are neurally in sync with the brain's negativity bias. Because of our historical preoccupation with the doctrine of original sin, we have in so many ways lost sight of the forest for the trees, the original beauty and goodness of creation and by extension the positivity of our own original worth and value as human beings created in God's image. All of this is reminiscent of Terrence Malick's film, *The Tree of Life* (2011), which is really a hymn to the grandeur and splendor of creation ever before us that we so often lose sight of because of a tunnel vision with what is wrong with us, the world, and with life. It leads one of the aging characters to lament at the end of the film, with deep pain and a profound sense of regret, "I dishonored it all and didn't notice the glory."

The same can be said of theology, not to mention psychology, that in our unwavering efforts to get to the bottom of what is wrong with us as human beings that we surely at times have overlooked the abundant blessings and glory that are forever around and within us. Perhaps the wisdom that we find in other religious traditions could be a guide in how we as pastoral and spiritual practitioners move forward, privileging once again the first creation story as the more defining narrative for human flourishing and the rebuilding of our positivity ratio. Tara Brach has already framed the issue as waking up from the trance of our assumed unworthiness, through an initial resolve and determination of the will, to be sure, but even more through the active daily practice of retraining the Western heart and mind. Additionally, Zen wisdom encourages an active return to our original nature, only it is the reverse of the theological construct of original sin. We discover, as we return again and again in spiritual practice to "the fundamental ground of our lives, our true human nature," that either "standing up, sitting down, laughing, weeping— these are jewels we don't recognize as our own treasure" (Bobrow, 2003, pp. 208–209). The ancient Zen teaching strikingly parallels that of Jesus, that the treasure of the kingdom of heaven is already present in each of us even if we do not always recognize it. As we attempt to center ourselves, contemplative-ly, in the simple and yet profound peace and joy of being, we find that it is ultimately unproductive to cling to any theology that encourages an aversion to human experience and existence. A direct encounter with the fullness of life and the fullness of our own humanity is what the Zen practitioner would call a "direct knowing," which requires a suspension of prior judgments about the problematic and originally sinful state of humanity. "This direct knowing is a passionate affair and we do well not to repeat the early tearing asunder of flesh and spirit that brought in its wake the body-mind split that we are only now revisioning" (Bobrow, 2003, pp. 208–209). In our daily contemplative-meditational practice, we return to the fundamental basis of our existence, only now we do so not by confessing our original sinfulness but rather by re-centering ourselves in the original goodness of God's creation. If we put this in neuroscientific terms, we will discover that the "revisioning" is being defined more and more by a path of spiritual awakening and an evolution of consciousness that "involves both transforming the mind/ brain and uncovering the wonderful true nature that was there all along" (Hanson, 2009, p. 19).

This is not at all to suggest that we naively bypass or gloss over, in Jungian terms, the human "shadow side," viewing human experience through a pair of rose-colored glasses or simply adopting a positive-thinking or mind-over-matter attitude. Nor is the Buddhist emphasis on basic and original goodness, what I am arguing is akin to the hidden treasure of the kingdom of God, an avoidance of the painful realities of human life. Writing in *Living Buddha, Living Christ*, Thich Nhat Hanh points out that "we do not speak about Original Sin in Buddhism, but we do talk about negative seeds that exist in every person—seeds of hatred, anger, ignorance, intolerance, and so on...." (2007, p. 44). The list could of course go on and on, only with one very important qualification: it is not human beings themselves, individually or collectively, or their basic original nature that is the problem. Rather, the fundamental issue is the present state of our development and our evolving emotional, psychological, and spiritual capacities that we see manifested attitudinally and behaviorally in everyday life. There are interesting parallels with the school of Rational Emotive Behavioral Therapy (REBT) put forward by Albert Ellis, which maintains the importance of always separating who people *are* from what they say or do or think. Ellis, in his years of clinical practice, was famously never one to look the other way when facing the "negative seeds" of human experience, although he did so in a way that purposely avoided co-mingling the specific negative actions and behaviors of his clients with any global meta-narrative about our nature or the human condition. Human beings, as Ellis discovered, for too long have had "a tendency to merge the action with the person or to evaluate a negative action with the whole person....your beliefs are rational so long as they do not make an evaluation of the *action* into an evaluation of the *person*" (2003, pp. 17–18). Similarly, to convert negative seeds of human thought and action into a totalizing theological discourse about human origins and nature is to confuse how we think and act with who we are. And, who we are by nature, according to the neuroscientist, the Buddhist teacher, the writer of the first creation story, and ultimately Jesus himself, is a unique creation of exceeding worth and value.

Once again, this is not meant to suggest a pollyannaish denial of the shadow side of human experience, the difficult realities and painful limitations of our individual and collective existence. The confession that we are originally good is simply, as Paul Ricoeur would see it, the dynamic and dialectical conflict of theological interpretations that opens the door to a necessary if not urgent re-prioritizing and re-privileging of theological categories. Otherwise, we are held hostage to theologies that keep us trapped in neural pathways of negativity, such as the Adamic myth of our innate sinfulness. But, this guiding myth, when viewed correlationally through the lens of neuroscience, is seen for what it really is, namely, more of a theological construct than an ontotheology. As Ricoeur has demonstrated, the Adamic myth, in its historical and even present shape and form, "culminates in the idea of a moral god conceived as the origin and foundation of an ethics of prohibition and condemnation" (2004, p. 443). For the neuroscientist, holding to this theological view can only strengthen and reinforce the deeply embedded negativity bias of the brain, something that is not conducive to our personal and collective growth and development as human beings. In many ways, we have through the help of neuroscience begun to outgrow the conceptualization of an innate sinfulness, whether attributed to the effects of guilty actions or to shameful feelings. We are, in other words, moving beyond the need for a theological construction of original sin and a moral god that would condemn us for not being further along in our collective and evolutionary development, ultimately through no fault of our own. Arguing with razor-sharp theological and psychological clarity, Ricoeur helps us see that a theology of original wrongdoing is simply "a product and projection of our own weakness" (2004, p. 443).

THE TRANSFORMATION OF "PRIOR LEARNING"

That we are moving in certain ways beyond an original-sin framework does not mean that it will happen overnight; the negativity bias of the brain, reinforced by the powerful Adamic myth of our innate sinfulness, by now runs very deep in the brain. Indeed, to search joyfully for the hidden treasure located within the human heart and mind would not have made any sense to our very early ancestors trying to simply stay alive on the Serengeti, nor perhaps even to more recent ancestors situated in the throes of crisis and calamity with the collapse of the Roman Empire, the rapid spread of Black Death, and so on. As we continue to move forward, theologically, beyond a perceived need to assuage our guilt for any original wrongdoing, which as Ricoeur has noted is simply a product and projection of our own weakness, it

will be important to keep in mind that we are swimming against very powerful undercurrents in the brain and central nervous system. To center and re-
center ourselves in the peace and joy of God's loving presence through daily
contemplative-meditational practice will require considerable patience as
"we understand what we're up against and have some compassion for ourselves" (Hanson, 2009, p. 46). As we have already learned from the distinguished work of Joseph LeDoux, this state of affairs is simply a reflection of
our present level of collective human development, the price we pay for
having newly evolved higher-order capacities that are not yet fully integrated
into the brain:

> Our brain has not evolved to the point where the new systems that make
> complex thinking possible can easily control the old systems that give rise to
> our base needs and motives, and emotional reactions. This does not mean that
> we are simply victims of our brains and should just give in to our urges. It
> means that downward causation is sometimes hard work....That the self is
> synaptic can be a curse—it doesn't take much to break it apart. But it is also a
> blessing, as there are always new connections waiting to be made (2002, pp.
> 322–324).

Making these new connections presupposes an intentional reordering of the
contents of the mind, as we seek to identify specific mental constructs, theological and psychological, that even partially impede our experiencing the
abundance and fullness of life. It is not at all surprising that the second
creation story, along with the theological idea that we are innately flawed and
sinful, has been privileged for so long and for so many centuries, given what
we are learning about the brain's built-in negativity bias. It is after all our
"normal" baseline at this moment of our individual and collective development, or in the words of Edmund Husserl, it is the "natural standpoint"
(Kockelmans, 1994, p. 122) that we automatically take for granted as corresponding to ultimate reality. However, as we have witnessed again and again
throughout history, a construct that may very well be "theologically true" in
its present shape and form is not always grounded in the reality of present-
moment lived experienced. In cognitive psychology, we would say that oftentimes a mental construction is assumed to be part of the very fabric of
reality, perhaps paralleling Freud's observation that "we assume that mental
life is the function of an apparatus to which we ascribe the characteristics of
being extended in space..." (1964/1940, p. 140). If we look closely at the
unambiguous findings of neuroscience, we will see that it is rather difficult to
embrace a construct of original guilt and sinfulness, either theological and/or
psychological, and at the same time experience any lasting feeling of peace
and joy. The difficulty is that while many pastoral and clinical practitioners
are trying to blaze healthier and more life-affirming pathways for themselves
and those in their care, to continue to confess an original sinfulness neu-

tralizes or in some cases even cancels out any neural progress that we are making in this direction. As we have learned, the "bad stuff" or the negative seeds of human experience are more deeply rooted in our psychology and physiology, and will therefore have more visceral force and resonance even if we are firmly committed to a life of spiritual growth and development. Put more simply, we cannot have our cake and eat it too, for as much as we want to believe that we are on the path leading to abundant life and to spiritual awakening, the sobering truth that we learn from neuroscience is that in continuing to privilege the second creation story over the first simply reinforces the brain's negativity bias. Because habituated ways of thinking and knowing, which presuppose that we are insufficient, flawed, or defective, run unusually deep in the Western mind and brain, awakening from the trance of our unworthiness in order to experience more fully the fundamental peace and joy of being must be supported by theological and psychological paradigms and epistemologies that encourage this transformational shift.

The paradigmatic turn begins with a very clear understanding of the built-in negativity bias of the brain and, as we have seen, how certain theological constructs can become if we are not careful potential impediments to our spiritual growth and development. More conscious of the neural terrain, we are freer to move into the active rewiring of the mind and brain through contemplative-meditational practice. Recall the neuroscientific data that illustrate rather compellingly the capacity of daily contemplative prayer and meditation to rewire the neural pathways in the brain, perhaps more effectively than any other medium. The reality of neuroplasticity, "the brain's capacity to learn—and thus change itself" (Hanson, 2009, p. 72), demonstrates that it is indeed possible for us and those in our care to grow and change across the lifespan provided we learn to transform the negative constructions of the mind. Change, not only to brain functioning but even more to the very structures of the brain, can certainly occur if we are actively and contemplatively engaged in the resculpting of neural pathways and if we are realistic about and patient with the process. So often in my pastoral and clinical practice, I will hear those in my care remark that they want to change negative patterns of thought and behavior right away and for good, without stopping to remember that even for St. Paul this was not entirely possible. Paul captures rather well the human condition, when he laments his misdeeds of commission and his errors of omission, something that surely resonates with all of us, practitioners and clients/congregants alike, if we are emotionally and spiritually honest. What neuroscience teaches us is that change does not happen overnight, that on a daily basis it is hardly noticeable, but over time if we are intentionally using the mind to rewire the brain it can and does occur. It is important to keep in mind that as we engage in the regular practice of contemplative prayer and meditation, any changes in neural structure and functioning will be mostly undetectable day by day. But, as Newberg demonstrated with the Franciscan nuns, the tiny and barely noticeable changes that occur on a daily basis will in fact add up as the years go by. Thus, with a certain resolve and determination we can through a daily spiritual practice begin to rewire the mind and brain in simple yet very profound ways. In so doing, we ground ourselves again and again in the extraordinary gift of the present moment, worrying and ruminating less about tomorrow and the future.

It is important to recall that Newberg's study of the nuns was longitudinal in nature, as they engaged in the daily practice of the Centering Prayer for a minimum of fifteen years. In all likelihood there were days for these contemplative practitioners, as with anyone else who engages regularly in daily prayer and meditation, when they would become distracted by anxious thoughts, feelings, and memories. What is important, according to Fr. Thomas Keating, is that we do not launch into judging ourselves in the process for any "obstacles caused by the hyperactivity of our mind and of our lives" (1994, p. 11). Rather than conclude that this is further evidence of our inherently flawed human nature, the nuns would simply re-center themselves in the peace and joy of the present moment and therefore over time were developing more healthful neural connections in the brain. In the language of Siegel, the nuns, through the daily practice of the Centering Prayer, were harnessing the power of mindful awareness, which can only occur if there is a "dissolution of the influences of prior learning" and a full immersion in the "state of 'nonjudging' experience" (2007, p. 134). As we develop a mindful awareness in the context of our contemplative-meditational practices, "the flow of energy and information that is our mind enters our conscious attention and we can both appreciate its contents and also come to regulate its flow in a new way" (Siegel, 2007, p. 5). The dissolution of prior learning in this case would be the view that we are inherently sinful; we become more mindful of its residual content and learn to disengage from its totalizing flow, grounding ourselves in the simple yet profound experience of being. Siegel puts it this way:

> Mindfulness heightens the capacity to become filled by the senses of the moment and attuned to our own state of being. As we also become aware of our awareness, we can sharpen our focus on the present, enabling us to feel our feet as we travel the path of our lives. We engage with ourselves and with others, making a more authentic connection, with more reflection and consideration. Life becomes more enriched as we are aware of the extraordinary experience of being, of being alive, of living in this moment (2007, pp. 14–15).

Chapter Four

Calming the Anxious Mind and Brain

The faculty of voluntarily bringing back a wandering attention over and over again, is the very root of judgment, character, and will...An education which should improve this faculty would be the education par excellence. —William James, *The Principles of Psychology*

Andrew Newberg's landmark study of the Franciscan nuns and the Buddhist monks engaged in the spiritual practices of, respectively, Centering Prayer and mindfulness meditation has revealed rather compelling that a daily contemplative-meditational practice "can make profound and permanent changes in our consciousness and our fundamental perceptions of the world" by enhancing memory, cognition, and attentiveness while lessening our stress (Newberg, 2009, p. 190). While prayer and meditation have long been recognized by various faith traditions as being religiously and spiritually beneficial, it has only been in recent years that we are beginning to see that the benefits are much broader and more multifaceted. Thus, while we would do well to continue focusing on the spirituality of prayer and meditation in the context of pastoral and spiritual care, it is becoming equally important in an age of heightened anxiety to have a better grasp of the physiological impact of contemplative-meditational practices on the mind and body. Neuroscientific studies are revealing that the daily practice of Centering Prayer and/or mindfulness meditation does have, above and beyond promoting spiritual growth and development, "a number of health benefits such as decreasing anxiety, depression, irritability and moodiness, and improving learning ability, memory, self-actualization, feelings of vitality and rejuvenation, and emotional stability" (Newberg, 2010, p. 206). Later in this chapter I will be presenting specific examples of contemplative prayer and meditation that if practiced with sufficient regularity will lend themselves over time to the cultivation of greater health and well-being in everyday life. Put another way, contemplative-meditational practices will increase our capacity for spiritual growth even as they simultaneously enhance the neurocircuitry that "helps a variety of medical conditions, strengthens the immune system, and improves psychological functioning" (Hanson, 2009, p. 96).

THE PHYSIOLOGICAL BENEFITS OF CONTEMPLATIVE SPIRITUAL PRACTICE

In 1975, the cardiologist Herbert Benson published what has become a classic in the field of mind-body research: *The Relaxation Response*. In the book, Benson put forward a simple meditative technique comprised of four basic elements, designed to lower the human individual's level of stress and anxiety. If practiced regularly enough, the meditative technique of finding a *quiet environment*, selecting an *object to dwell upon*, cultivating a *passive attitude*, and assuming a *comfortable position* will elicit the "relaxation response" that can help to balance the corrosive effects of an overstressed life (Benson, 1975, pp. 78–79). It should be noted that the third element of the technique, developing a "passive" attitude, is something of a misnomer, for the elicitation of the relaxation response requires more of an active awareness than it does any sort of passive mindset. The third element, more precisely, has to do with the fostering of an open and spacious awareness of the varied contents of the mind, including any thoughts, feelings, memories, and so forth. When engaged, for example, in mindfulness meditation and/or daily Centering Prayer, our initial goal is admirably to dwell in the immediacy of the present moment as well as in the fullness of God's loving presence. But before too long distracting thoughts and feelings will inevitably drift into our awareness like shooting stars in the night sky, prompting us if amygdala-driven to think about and in many cases ruminate about tomorrow and the next day and the day after that. Rather than getting "hijacked" by distracting thoughts or feelings, either in the form of letting them consume our attention while trying to meditate and/or fighting with and trying to repress them, we develop a passive, i.e., an open attitude that can observe the contents of the mind as if they were simply passing clouds or shooting stars in the sky. I will have more to say about the importance of an open and non-judgmental awareness of our experience, as we engage in contemplative spiritual practices, when we get to the next section of this chapter. For as Benson had noted decades ago, and this continues to be supported by more recent contemplative neuroscience, it is this element of the meditative and prayerful technique more than any other that has the capacity to elicit an increased feeling of relaxation in the present moment combined with lowering the level of our stress and anxiety (1975, p. 79).

Benson's work has been pioneering in terms of mind-body research and more specifically in the neuroscientific study of the physiology of prayer and meditation. In fact, as Newberg points out, contemplative neuroscience clearly owes a debt of gratitude to Benson, who through dozens of carefully designed studies "demonstrated that you could consciously reduce stress and tension throughout your body by breathing slowly and repeating a word or phrase that gives you a sense of comfort (God, peace, etc.)" (Newberg, 2009, p. 45). The meditative focus on a meaningful word or phrase or mantra, combined with a comfortable and quiet setting and an attitude of open awareness, clearly parallels, as we will see later in the chapter, the contemplative method of Centering Prayer put forward by Fr. Thomas Keating. For now, it is important to recall that a daily spiritual practice has the potential to alter both the functioning *and* the structure of the neural networks of the brain, so that over time the brain of someone regularly engaged in contemplative prayer and meditation will differ from someone else not engaged in these daily practices. More specifically, as Richard Davidson has found, the regular practice of contemplative prayer and meditation "not only produces distinct patterns of brain activity in real time but also leaves enduring changes in that activity—so that the brain of a meditator is different from that of a nonmeditator even when she is not meditating" (2012, p. 196). For the nuns and Buddhist monks in Newberg's study, the key difference was an increase in the executive or higher-order functions of brain activity and a decrease in limbic activity associated with amygdala-driven vigilance and reactivity, which generates a deeper and more lasting sense of peace and contentment. Meditation can therefore be thought of as "a top-down approach, beginning with the images in the brain which then influence brain and body responses through the limbic system and ultimately the brain stem" (Hogue, 2003, p. 150). Neuroscientific studies continue to reveal that a daily contemplative-meditational practice produces tangible physiological, psychological, social, relational, and not to mention, spiritual benefits. Newberg points out that even if we take the most conservative assessment from numerous medical, neurological, and psychological studies, we can easily draw the following conclusion:

> Activities involving meditation and intensive prayer permanently strengthen neural functioning in specific parts of the brain that are involved with lowering anxiety and depression, enhancing social awareness and empathy, and improving cognitive and intellectual functioning. The neural circuits activated by meditation buffer us from the deleterious effects of aging and stress and give us better control over our emotions. At the very least, such practices help us remain calm, serene, peaceful, and alert. And for nearly everyone, it gives a positive and optimistic outlook on life (2009, pp. 149–150).

Whereas the spirituality of prayer and meditation has received much attention through the centuries, it is only recently that we are beginning to more
fully understand the physiological benefits of contemplative and meditational
practices. For example, Sara W. Lazar, in extensively researching the neurobiology of meditation at Massachusetts General Hospital and Harvard Medical School, by way of functional magnetic resonance imaging, or fMRI, has
consistently demonstrated for more than a decade that "regular meditation
practice literally reshapes one's brain, leading to long-lasting changes in
neural function" (2013, p. 291). What we are learning, in other words, is that
a "regular" spiritual practice, to use Lazar's word, can and will change the
structure and functioning of the brain for the better by altering neural networks and synaptic connections. More specifically, contemplative-meditational practice has the twofold benefit of enhancing and strengthening areas
of the brain related to compassion and empathy while minimizing "the power
of the portion of the brain that controls fear, anxiety, and anger" (Snyderman,
2011, pp. 179–180). The result is a fundamental alteration of the neural
structures involved in fear and anxiety, albeit incremental from day to day
and yet as we have seen in Newberg's research a more transformational
alteration can occur over time. Moreover, what develops is a widening of
what Siegel calls a "window of tolerance," the increasing capacity to "maintain equilibrium in the face of stresses that would once have thrown us off
kilter" (2011, p. 137). In cultivating a daily rhythm of contemplative prayer
and/or mindfulness meditation, we build up through the months and years the
neural structure that supports our capacity to remain emotionally grounded
and spiritually centered even in the midst of anxious times and stressful
circumstances. And, as the window of tolerance widens, we experience more
fully the "power of the pause" (Brach, 2003, p. 68) which is the gateway to
monitoring and modulating our anxious awareness and reactivity triggered
by a hypervigilant amygdala. This has important implications for moving
beyond a mere intellectual grasp of Jesus' teaching on anxiety, as we help
those in our care develop practical methods for putting his words into practice in everyday life.

The widening window of tolerance that we develop through contemplative-meditational practices creates the necessary space where, as we learned
earlier from Siegel, we can harness the power of mindful awareness in order
to decouple automaticity and create the essential pause of emotional, social,
and spiritual intelligence. Neuroscience has revealed that a daily spiritual
practice can help us actually "focus our minds in a way that changes the
structure and function of the brain throughout our lives," which will yield
"neurologic and immune improvements" (Siegel, 2007, p. 96). Additionally,
we can learn in our daily practice to calm the amygdala-hippocampus structures of the limbic region that keep us ever vigilant and on edge, even when
anxious awareness is not warranted. On the one hand, there is nothing new

under the sun in that for centuries we have known that it is in our best interests not to worry about tomorrow, even if there has been confusion about how to put this spiritual teaching into everyday practice. On the other hand, what is new is the discovery of neuroplasticity, which reveals specific ways that we can maintain our balance and equilibrium in the present moment and let tomorrow worry about itself. Being aware of the present moment without grasping onto worries about the future "offers a powerful path toward both compassion and inner well-being," something that "science verifies and what has been taught over thousands of years of [spiritual] practice" (Siegel, 2007, p. 96). A contemplative approach to religious faith and even life in general for that matter enhances our capacity to live more fully in the present moment, the difference between living "mindfully" and living "mindlessly" on automatic pilot. Living on automatic pilot puts us at "risk of mindlessly reacting to situations without reflecting on various options of response." Siegel continues:

> The result can often be knee-jerk reactions that in turn initiate similar mindless reflexes in others. A cascade of reinforcing mindlessness can create a world of thoughtless interactions, cruelty, and destruction....By bringing the individual closer to a deep sense of his or her own inner world, it offers the opportunity to enhance compassion and empathy. Mindfulness is not "self-indulgent," it is actually a set of skills that enhances the capacity for caring relationships with others (2007, p. 14).

We can still draw the conclusion that daily prayer and meditation is good for us, only now neuroscience has equipped us with a more multidimensional understanding of the benefits. While meditational practices, as we have known for centuries, enhance our spiritual growth and development, they also as we are discovering foster physiological and psychological health and well-being. To put it another way, spiritual practices were primarily designed to strengthen our religious faith, deepen our connection with God and other human beings, and ultimately lead us toward spiritual enlightenment and transformation, rather than for the purpose of fostering physiological and psychological health and well-being. And yet, as Newberg discovered with his neuroimaging studies of the nuns and monks, there is something quite different about the brain engaged in the daily practice of Centering Prayer and/or mindfulness meditation that correlates positively with physiological growth and development. He points out that when compared to the normal baseline of everyday awareness, the brain during meditational practice operates in a distinctly unique and even unusual way that reflects permanent changes in consciousness and fundamental perceptions of life and the world, increased social cooperation and cognitive performance, and enhanced memory and attentiveness (Newberg, 2009, pp. 190–191). It therefore becomes important for those of us working in the field of pastoral and spiritual care to broaden our understanding of the health benefits associated with various spiritual practices, in order to increase our overall effectiveness with anxious congregants and clients. Again, this will necessitate something of a paradigm shift away from a primary focus on religious beliefs and doctrine with a secondary focus on contemplative spiritual practice toward an approach that elevates the latter to a level of comparable importance with the former. The paradigm shift, to be sure, reflects a growing understanding of the latest findings from neuroscientific research, which when combined with the spiritual wisdom already inherent in our religious faith traditions will lead to more informed and effective interventions with those in our care. For example, along with the awareness that contemplative prayer and meditation is spiritually beneficial, guiding us toward a deeper experience of the peace of God that transcends human understanding, pastoral and spiritual caregivers now have the knowledge that mindfulness-based meditational practices, such as the Centering Prayer of the Franciscan nuns, can and do "help people with depression, anxiety, high blood pressure, psoriasis, trauma, eating disorders, substance abuse, and a variety of psychopathological behaviors" (Newberg, 2009, p. 191).

The neuroscientific findings regarding the physiology of meditation highlight the human brain's extraordinary untapped potential, that through various contemplative practices we have the opportunity to change the functioning, organization, and anatomical structure of our own brain. This is the promise of neuroplasticity, whereby the neurons that we intentionally fire together in the context of our daily spiritual practice will begin to wire or rewire together in positive and life-affirming ways. Specific meditation exercises or techniques that lend themselves to the resculpting of neural pathways and structures include, but are not limited to, the Centering Prayer of Fr. Thomas Keating that was practiced by the nuns in Newberg's study, which focuses on a sacred word or mantra; mindfulness breathing that as Benson and others since him have discovered triggers a feeling of relaxation in the brain; walking meditation, which facilitates engagement with the world of God's creation and a deeper respect and gratitude for it; and guided meditation, in which we visualize or imagine ourselves, for example, in a peaceful and relaxing place, in God's abiding and loving presence, more meaningfully connected to loved ones or friends, experiencing a positive outcome to a difficult experience, and so forth. A guided form of meditation can also focus on the expansion of compassionate awareness, toward a part of ourselves that we struggle with or even against, toward a difficult neighbor or colleague, toward a friend or loved one, and ultimately to all of humankind. Davidson, in his research, has discovered that those engaged in regular compassion meditation show striking changes in brain function, most notably a decrease or reduction in amygdala activity (2012, p. 222). This has unique relevance for helping those in our care manage their anxiety in a world where we are still taught to think in either-or categories of us versus them, to fear those who are "different," to suspiciously assume the worst about the other's intentions, all of it amygdala-driven. Compassion meditation, as Davidson has found, reduces personal fear and distress, so that people who practice it regularly "develop a strong disposition to alleviate suffering and to wish others to be happy" (2012, p. 223).

From the standpoint of neuroscience, what makes meditation practices effective is that they quiet specific limbic regions of the brain, in particular they can turn down the volume of the amygdala. Over time, this allows for the expansion of consciousness and greater perceptual clarity, generating a more spacious and panoramic awareness of the totality of life. So often we and those in our care get trapped in a tunnel vision of negativity and vigilance, triggered and fueled by excessive amygdala activity. A regular spiritual practice helps us quiet down the disproportionate limbic activity, freeing us to see, so to speak, more of the spacious forest for all the trees. For example, we learn to "step back" and observe the totality of our experience, including our negative thoughts and anxious feelings, without getting "hijacked" or "hooked." I will have more to say about this all-too-familiar process of get ting hooked by the contents of the mind when we look at mindfulness therapeutic approaches in the next chapter. In the context of mindfulness meditation we "observe our own thoughts and feelings moment to moment and without judgment, from the perspective of a third party" (Davidson, 2012, p. 132). A useful metaphor is to observe our negative thoughts and anxious feelings as passing clouds in the spacious sky, which as we know from meteorology are here today at this moment but by tomorrow or even later today will have faded away. In so doing, we create what Davidson refers to as new and different neural pathways or channels—"much as water that had always followed one path along a stream can be diverted to a different course after a sudden storm, for instance, carving a new channel" (2012, pp. 204–205). Engaging in the regular practice of contemplative prayer and meditation can and will over time carve out new pathways or channels in the "streambeds" of the mind and brain. As Davidson notes, the more our thoughts travel along the neural paths of less anxiety, the greater our resilience and positivity will be, making "it easier for thoughts and feelings to continue taking this route" (2012, p. 205). He illustrates the benefits of mindfulness meditation with a practical example from everyday life:

> Whereas the thought of how much you need to accomplish tomorrow (driving the children to school; going to an important meeting for work; getting a plumber to fix the leak under the sink; calling the IRS about the mistake they caught on your 1040; getting dinner on the table…) used to trigger a panicky sense of being overwhelmed, mindfulness sends thoughts through a new culvert: You still think about all you have to do, but when the sense of being overwhelmed kicks in, you regard that thought with dispassion. You think,

*Well of course the sense of being overwhelmed is starting to course through
my brain,* but you step back from it and let it go, realizing that allowing it to
hijack your brain will not help. Mindfulness retrains these habits of mind by
tapping into the plasticity of the brain's connections, creating new ones,
strengthening some old ones, and weakening others (2012, p. 205).

CULTIVATING NON-JUDGMENTAL AWARENESS

The third-party observation of our thoughts, feelings, and sensations during
the practice of prayer and meditation, a sort of transcendent awareness of the
totality of our experience, is a fundamental prerequisite to creating new
connections and pathways in the brain. This harks back to Benson's research
on the relaxation response and his discovery that above all else the cultivation of a "passive attitude" vis-à-vis the totality of our experience is necessary for lowering stress and anxiety. During the practice of Centering Prayer
and/or mindfulness meditation, for example, we do *not* judge our performance or how well we are doing, nor do we keep track of how often our
mind wanders with distracting thoughts or feelings. If we are engaged in a
twenty-minute Centering Prayer meditation, perhaps repeating the mantra of
Jesus from the Sermon on the Mount ("Do not be anxious"), we will soon
notice that anxious thoughts and feelings come to mind: What will I make for
dinner? Am I prepared for today's meeting? Did the kids do their homework?
But rather than letting ourselves lose our meditational focus, either by in-
dulging the distracting thought or fighting with it, we simply *and* gently
bring our awareness back to the anchoring mantra without any need for
critique. As Benson made clear, this meditational trajectory is "normal" for
most of us; anxious and distracting thoughts are to be expected and do not
mean that we are not getting it right or that we are less spiritual than the other
person. The passive attitude that parallels Davidson's third-party observation
is a "let it happen" attitude of non-judgmental awareness, which for Benson
and other researchers since him is the most important meditational element in
calming the hyperactivity of the mind. As we develop and cultivate a daily
spiritual practice, it is most important to remember that it is counterproductive to "worry about how well we are performing the technique, because this
may well prevent the Relaxation Response from occurring" (Benson, 1975,
p. 113).

In chapter one we learned from Newberg that the worst thing we can do in
the context of daily prayer and meditation is to critically judge our performance, for the self-criticism will trigger amygdala-hippocampus reactions
that in turn will release no shortage of stress-provoking neurochemicals. As
Newberg puts it, it will not take long for any of us to discover in the quietude
of our meditation that "there is a critical voice inside all of us that is constantly judging every little thing that we do" (2009, p. 195). Coming face to face

with the so-called "inner critic" is therefore to be expected in any form of meditational practice, for it is perhaps the definitive internal manifestation of the brain's negativity bias, "In meditation, as in therapy, we learn to watch our negativity and not react to it," to be more "accepting of who we are, of our weaknesses as well as strengths" (Newberg, 2009, pp. 40 & 195). Moreover, as we learned from Siegel's research, our efforts to combat the distracting thoughts and feelings that enter our awareness only creates more amygdala-driven internal tension, a self-inflicted distress that will ultimately amplify rather than lower the mental chatter. A third-party awareness of the way we are sometimes a slave to the expectations and judgments of the inner critic creates the necessary space and distance where we can begin to disengage from identifying with any of the self-accusations and criticisms. Siegel reminds us that trying to banish a negative thought or feeling by resolutely ordering ourselves to do so is a strategy that will get us nowhere; physiologically, the internal "battle" with ourselves only reinforces the neurocircuitry supporting the negativity. This is not to suggest that "anything goes," as if a mindful and non-judgmental awareness of our thoughts, feelings, attitudes, and moods means that we are destined to act upon them. Cultivating an open and non-judgmental awareness of the totality of our experience as it *is* rather than how we think it *should be* simply opens the door to "accepting what is and not being swept up by those judging activities." Siegel further points out that in the context of our meditational practice,

> Rather than march into our inner world and say "No—don't do that!" we can embrace what is and notice what happens. Amazingly, time after time people discover that letting things be also allows them to change. We can approach our inner world with openness and acceptance rather than with judgments and preconceptions....But to get to this place of inner attunement, of internal acceptance, we must first become aware of when we are our own prison wardens (2011, pp. 97–98).

As a way to frame this in the context of our daily spiritual practice, not to mention in our everyday lives, Siegel offers the useful acronym of COAL, which stands for curiosity, openness, acceptance, and love. If, for example, we are meditating on the mantra, "Do not be anxious about tomorrow," or "Be still and know that I am God," or "God is love," and a disturbing thought, anxious feeling, and/or painful memory comes to mind, we do not indulge it or fight with it because either way this is to let the mental distractions hijack our present-moment experience. The disturbing thought might have to do with the implications of being unemployed, the anxious feeling of whether our child will make it through college or not, the painful memory of ending a marriage, the loss of a loved one. At one extreme, we might be tempted to turn our meditational time into a spiritual battle, to march into our inner world and fire off the order, "No—don't do that," for this is after all our time to be fully in the presence of God. At the other extreme, we allow and become so preoccupied with or "hooked" by the thought or feeling that before we know it we are unmoored and adrift in what was to be a centering start to the day. The latter is NOT what Siegel means by being curious, open, and accepting, for this kind of attachment and preoccupation will only stimulate the neural pathways that reinforce the brain's negativity bias. Rather, the COAL approach to contemplative-meditational practice and even to life in general has to do with cultivating a mindful and reflective awareness of the totality of one's experience in the present moment, a meta-awareness of our awareness as it were. "This distinction between awareness with COAL and just paying attention with preconceived ideas that imprison the mind, ("I shouldn't have hit my foot, I'm so clumsy," "Why did I fall off this cliff? What is wrong with me!") is the difference between being aware, and being mindfully aware" (Siegel, 2007, p. 16).

In the context of our daily spiritual practice, which inevitably will be flooded with distracting thoughts and feelings at one time or another, the preconceived ideas may sound more like, "I'm a failure at this!," "What difference does it make?", or "Who am I kidding, I'll never be good at this!" But as we have learned, what is most counterproductive is to judge ourselves and our meditational performance and spiritual progress, for this will only fire up the amygdala that in turn will increase our stress and anxiety. Siegel further clarifies the COAL approach to mindful awareness, whether we are specifically engaged in meditational practice or with everyday life:

> Cultivating mindful awareness requires that we become aware of awareness *and* that we be able to notice when those "top-down" preconceptions of shoulds and ought-to's are choking us from living mindfully. ...*Top-down* refers to the way that our memories, beliefs, and emotions shape our "bottom-up" direct sensation of experience. Kindness to ourselves is what gives us the strength and resolve to break out of that top-down prison and approach life's events, planned or unplanned, with curiosity, openness, acceptance, and love. ...I am proposing here that mindful awareness is a form of self-relationship, an internal form of attunement that creates similar states of health. This may be the as yet unidentified mechanism by which mindfulness promotes well-being (2007, pp. 16–17).

Siegel's application of COAL (curiosity, openness, acceptance, and love) to spiritual practice and to life in general in certain ways parallels another mindfulness tool put forward by Tara Brach under the acronym, RAIN. During our practice of contemplative prayer and meditation, distracting thoughts, anxious feelings, and/or painful memories will certainly appear from time to time as if out of nowhere, without any warning. This is normal and to be expected; it does not mean that we are doing our spiritual practices wrong or that we are not as spiritual as we thought we were. Rather than fight to repress or keep the lid on the contents of the mind or conversely to get lost in ruminating about this thought or that feeling, all of which only serves to reinforce the negativity circuitry of the brain, we simply Recognize what is happening in any given moment, Allow and "let be" whatever is arising in the present moment, Investigate our inner experience with compassion and curiosity rather than with fear and judgment, and through Non-identification with any passing sensation, emotion, or thought to find rest in the liberating realization of our natural and God-given awareness (Brach, 2012, pp. 62–65). To be curious, open, and accepting of the totality of our inner experience, to recognize, allow, and investigate all of it without fear and judgment may seem a bit counterintuitive for some pastoral and spiritual caregivers. After all, Judeo-Christian theology has at times framed the human condition and our human existence in a less than favorable light, that we are inherently and originally sinful. Recall from last chapter John Calvin's rather graphic description of our inner experience, going so far as to describe it as a world of miseries and horde of infamies. While most clergy and pastoral practitioners would not use such excessively graphic and pejorative language in today's faith communities, the tendency to judge ourselves as inherently flawed and originally sinful still lingers. In my own faith tradition, for example, we still feel a compelling need to confess our sinful condition at the beginning of every Sunday service before we can offer our worship, praise, and thanksgiving to God. Up to a point, this has the benefit of keeping us emotionally and spiritually honest, personally and collectively, of identifying weaknesses and areas of growth within ourselves and within our communities that need our ongoing attention. That said, the downside is that a theology of innate sinfulness, taken at face value and manifested in the persistent need to judge our inner world of thoughts, feelings, and sensations, can and will trigger amygdala-hippocampus reactions in the brain that ultimately keep us on edge and feeling anxious. This can only leave us in a state of neural, not to mention spiritual fragmentation, which is a serious impediment to the fostering of neuroplasticity and to experiencing more fully the joy and peace of God's presence.

It is important to remember that a non-judgmental stance toward the varied contents of the mind correlates with a reduction of activity in the amygdala. As we reduce this activity through contemplative and mindfulness meditational practices, the brain can become more habituated to "perceiving thoughts, emotions, and sensations less judgmentally and less hysterically, so that we are not hijacked by our internal chatter" (Davidson, 2012, p. 235). As we have already discussed, it is useful to imagine or think about the varied contents of our experience metaphorically, for example, as clouds in a very spacious daytime sky that are here one moment and gone the next. Or, we can imagine the contents of the mind and the feeling tones of experience as shooting stars in the nighttime sky, coming and going all the time. We see the daytime cloud or the nighttime shooting star, and then we go back to what we were doing before: reading our book, talking to a friend or loved one, watching television, returning to our sacred word and mantra. The spaciousness and boundlessness of awareness "allows every content of mind to be or not to be, to come and go—dwarfing them, untroubled by them, unaffected by their passing" (Hanson, 2009, p. 115). Additionally, it can be useful to imagine distracting thoughts or anxious feelings as waves in a vast ocean of water, the normal and perpetual rhythm of ebb and flow in human life. As we engage in meditational practices, we "pressure test our attention in order to strengthen it—precisely because it goes against the grain of the tendencies we evolved to survive" (Hanson, 2009, p. 192). The internal mental chatter that arises in the quiet of our meditation time is not our fault or a reflection of any personal failure, as if the constant ebbing and flowing of mental contents and feeling tones reflects our inability to "get it right" when it comes to religious faith and spiritual practice. Rather, as we learned in chapter two, the persistent internal chatter and hyperactivity of the mind is simply the vestige of an earlier human brain designed to keep us alive at all costs.

As we develop a regular contemplative-meditational rhythm, we strengthen the neural connections between the prefrontal cortex and the amygdala, fostering an equanimity that will keep us more emotionally balanced and spiritually grounded. The amygdala becomes, so to speak, more accountable to the higher-order executive functions of the brain, and is therefore less likely to have free reign driving wave after wave of anxious thoughts and feelings. Moreover, spiritual practices can weaken the chain of amygdala-hippocampus reactions that keep us obsessing and in certain cases catastrophizing about a challenging experience or set of circumstances. "As soon as our thoughts begin to leap from one catastrophe to the next in this chain of woe, we have the mental wherewithal to pause, observe how easily the mind does this, note that it is an interesting mental process, and resist getting drawn into the abyss" (Davidson, 2012, p. 243). Learning to do this presupposes a certain "observational distance that allows us to watch our own mental activity," to learn to "sit" in the higher-order functioning of the prefrontal cortex and "not get swept up by the brain waves crashing in on [us] from other neural regions" (Siegel, 2011, p. 95). The observational distance, to be sure, reflects a non-judgmental meta-awareness of our experience in the present moment, manifested in the qualities of curiosity, openness, acceptance, and love (COAL). It is a moment-to-moment awareness that takes each thought or feeling or sensation as it comes, a compassionate awareness of the totality of our experience. The "non-judgmental" part, according to Davidson, is key: If, for example, we are engaged in contemplative prayer and our legs begin to feel tense, we do not criticize or scold ourselves for having difficulty relaxing; "our reaction is closer to 'Huh, tense legs; interesting'." He continues:

By learning to observe non-judgmentally, we can break the chain of associations that typically arise from every thought. *Ugh, I have to stop worrying about work* becomes *Oh, how interesting that a thought about problems at work has entered my consciousness, Ouch, my knee is killing me* becomes *Aha, a signal from my knee has reached my brain.* If these observations start spinning off into judgmental thoughts, as they tend to do (*I should have finished that project sooner than two minutes before the deadline!*), try to return to the process of mere observation. Developing these mindful habits often takes considerable practice, though our research indicates that even short amounts of time can make a difference. Many people report benefits after just twenty minutes of practice (2012, pp. 201 & 235).

CONTEMPLATIVE-MEDITATIONAL PRACTICES

There are many contemplative practices and meditational techniques that can help us live more fully and abundantly in the present moment, rather than anxiously focusing on tomorrow and the future. Before offering some examples, it is important to correct an assumption that some of us may have about the central purpose of meditation. Ironically, some colleagues in the field of pastoral ministry and pastoral counseling have asked me more than once, "Isn't meditation an escape from 'real life'?", or "Doesn't it distract us from the hard realities of life?" No doubt this limited view is fed by stereotypes and caricatures of meditators, "sitting and blissing out under a mango tree in order to have a better day" (Ricard, 2011, p. 25). I would argue that the view of contemplative life and practice representing something of a departure from the more central religious foci of liturgical practice, theology, and a focus on church teachings, perhaps even a luxury for the devoted few, betrays a lack of firsthand experience with a regular spiritual practice. Whether we are focused more on the spirituality of contemplative practices or, like the neuroscientist, focused more on the psychophysiological benefits of meditational techniques, either way what we are cultivating is *not* a blissful and escapist detachment from life and the "real world" but rather a deeper and fuller engagement with it. We come into this world *already distracted*, predisposed to be on high alert with the external environment and even with our own internal experience, a distinct obstacle to living more abundantly and less anxiously in the present moment. A regular practice of contemplative prayer and meditation can begin to free us from the habitual and less mindful ways we so often relate to life, to others, and to our own experience. As such, it offers the potential for daily and long-term transformation, "becoming a better human being for one's own well-being and that of others as well" (Ricard, 2011, p. 25). For many of us, including pastoral and spiritual caregivers, it may seem counterintuitive at first because we are so hardwired to always be striving for something more and to be getting somewhere else as quickly as possible. But as Jon Kabat-Zinn has found in his work with mind-

fulness-based stress reduction, "meditation requires not trying to get some-
place else so much as being where we already are, thus non-striving." He
adds that

> Meditation is not merely a relaxation technique. It is not a technique at all, but
> a way of being and of seeing, resting on a foundation of deep inquiry into the
> nature of self, and offering the potential for liberation from the small-minded-
> ness of self-preoccupation. Often people will say… "Wait a minute! This isn't
> stress reduction; this is my whole life!" It is a moment of revelation (2011, pp.
> 40 & 43).

The important thing to keep in mind is that we find a daily meditational
practice that "works" for us, i.e., it is spiritually meaningful and has a deep
psychophysiological resonance for restoring equanimity and equilibrium in
our hearts and minds. For me, personally, I try to practice as much as possible the Centering-Prayer method of Fr. Keating, which helped to transform
the neural pathways of the Franciscan nuns in Newberg's study. According
to Davidson, this form of contemplative-meditational practice is "one-
pointed concentration," with the meditator focusing on a single object of
attention and thus "strengthening the attentional focus until he achieves a
tranquil state in which preoccupation with other thoughts and emotions is
gradually eliminated" (2012, p. 215). Not that we should attach ourselves to
the unrealistic expectation that a tranquil state can be achieved and sustained
once and for all, even for the twenty minutes of Centering Prayer, for as we
have learned the "mental chatter" of the mind will inevitably begin to intrude
and distract us from the sacred word or object that was the initial focus of our
attention. To briefly summarize the straightforward four-step method of Centering Prayer, (1) we find a relaxing place where we can sit comfortably, (2)
we choose a word or mantra that will be the sacred object of our attention for
the twenty minutes or more of contemplative prayer and meditation, (3) the
sacred object of attention symbolizes our intention to be fully present with
God, and (4) when we become distracted by any intruding thought (e.g., "Am
I ready for today's meeting at work?", "What will I have for lunch?", and so
on), we simply "return ever so gently to the sacred word as the gift of your
whole being to God present within you" (Keating, 2006, p. 122). Returning
ever so gently to the sacred object of attention and concentration is in keeping with the important finding of neuroscience: the more we can resist blam-
ing and criticizing ourselves for not doing the meditation correctly or "right,"
the more we will calm the amygdala and reduce the myriad stress-provoking
neurochemicals it produces. For Keating, the basic principle for handling
distracting thoughts is quite simple, though of course sometimes easier said
than done: By remembering to *ever so gently* return to our sacred word or
mantra whenever there is any mental chatter, we are able to "resist no

thought, retain no thought, and react emotionally to no thought" (Keating, 2006, p. 127).

For contemplative practitioners, the goal is not a detachment or disengagement from life but rather a deeper and fuller investment in a life that, as Merton has put it, is fully awake, fully active, and fully aware that it is abundantly alive. It is a daily practice of centering and re-centering in the gift of "now," the present moment and day that God has made, and ultimately parallels the spiritual approach of Jesus who after being fully engaged with the demands of his own life and ministry—preaching, teaching, healing, caring for the poor—goes away again and again to a solitary place in order to return more fully engaged with the fullness of life. The regular practice of contemplative prayer and meditation is, similarly for pastoral and spiritual caregivers and those in our care, "not simply navel-gazing, nor is it simply about God and you alone," for a daily centering and re-centering in the peace and joy of God's presence "will lead you to the rest of creation" (Martin, 2010, p. 165). Perhaps paradoxically, then, the daily practice of the Centering Prayer will help to guide us toward a deeper and more meaningful engagement with and investment in God's creation, as we learn to develop an observational distance from the contents of the mind that simply reinforce the brain's predisposition toward an anxious and fragmented awareness. In my own Centering Prayer practice, for example, I will focus on a beautiful Franciscan prayer as my mantra in those times when I am feeling most anxious and by extension less mindful of God's abiding and loving presence: "O my God, you are here; O my God, I am here; O my God, we are here, and always, always, always you love us" (In A. Jones, 2006, p. 56). For someone feeling burdened and overwhelmed by the demands of life, the mantra could be Jesus' words, "Come to me, all you who are weary and burdened, and I will give you rest" (Matthew 11:28), or the words of the psalmist, "Be still, and know that I am God (Psalm 46:10), or even the beautifully familiar words of the 23rd Psalm, "He makes me lie down in green pastures, He leads me beside quiet waters" (Psalm 23:2). "If you are a busy person—or feeling swamped—you might simply rest with God," for it is very possible that with the latter, lying down in green pastures and beside still waters, "all God wants to do in that prayer is to give you rest" (Martin, 2010, p. 160). For others the focus on a single word, such as "love," "peace," "joy," "mercy," or "God" may be sufficient to anchor one's awareness in the abiding reality of divine presence. Whatever the sacred word or mantra that resonates deeply for you or me in our daily practice, we must not forget that

> Centering Prayer is simple in theory. In practice, it can be difficult for beginners, especially if your life is packed with "content." The notion that you could meet God without "doing" anything may seem bizarre. But Centering Prayer is

not about producing or achieving. It is about being. Or rather, being with
(Martin, 2010, p. 167).

That said, the more we do it, the more we engage in the *practice* of contemplative prayer and meditation, the more it becomes "second nature," a way of
being rather than an effortful task and undertaking that we feel we *should* do.
No matter where we start, even if we are a "beginner," we can, through the
regular practice of focusing on a sacred word and/or mantra that has deep
meaning and resonance, begin to harness the power of mindful awareness. In
certain ways, as we have suggested before, it becomes analogous to a regular
exercise or workout routine at the gym. The mindful awareness that we
cultivate through meditational practice is similarly "like a muscle: when we
use it, it gets stronger" (Hanson, 2009, p. 200). This is more than a specula-
tive hunch, for it is based on, in the words of Gazzaniga, the neuroscientific
finding that the "naturally developing automaticity of newly learned acts"
enhances brain plasticity. He likens the process to learning to ride a bike:

> It appears that the brain uses many brain cells (neurons) at first to carry out a
> task but that as the skill is learned, the number of neurons necessary for
> processing it becomes smaller and smaller. Similarly, when you first learn to
> ride a bike you need training wheels, but as you get better at the task you
> eventually wean yourself off them. The brain seems to work in a similar
> fashion....Researchers have elucidated how the brain whittles down the
> neurons as it learns a certain task and simplifies the brain response in such a
> way that the act becomes automatic—just like riding a bike (2005, p. 66).

As we intentionally use the mind to rewire the brain, we discover that over
time we are able to harness more of the power of mindful awareness, not only
in the context of daily prayer and meditation but increasingly in all areas of
our lives. The Centering-Prayer method, for example, lends itself to life in
general, so that one's sacred word or mantra can have a re-centering and
calming effect in anxious moments and stressful situations. When amygdala-
driven reactions are triggered by stressful circumstances at anytime of the
day, e.g., stuck in traffic on the way to an important event or meeting, having
a disagreement with a spouse or child, at a job interview or performance
review, and so forth, we can come back again and again to our sacred word
or mantra in order to re-center our anxious hearts and minds in the gift of the
present moment. The mindful awareness that we cultivate in the practice of
contemplative prayer and meditation is pivotal in "fostering a shift from a
transitory state to a more enduring and robust trait, a way of being grounded
in present-moment embodied experience rather than being caught in an elaborate cognitive self-narrative characteristic of depressive rumination, chronic
anxiety, daydreaming, and self-absorbed fantasizing" (Kabat-Zinn and Davidson, 2011b, p. 211). Through a regular centering practice, we build up new

neural, not to mention spiritual "muscle" that helps us remain grounded in the gift and joy of the present moment without getting hijacked by the "waves" of anxious thoughts and depressive feelings triggered by stressful circumstances. At the level of conscious experience, the practice of mindful awareness allows us to "see that it is possible to take a wholly different approach to the endless cycles of mental strategizing and affliction that are part and parcel of depression and anxiety" (Kabat-Zinn and Davidson, 2011b, p. 211).

The sacred word or mantra that is the focus of our contemplative prayer and meditation becomes an anchor, not only in the transitory state of our meditational practice itself but in the totality of our present-moment embodied experience. Contemplative-meditational practice, then, is not as we have already determined a detachment from the realities and practicalities of "real life," nor can it be a sidebar to other religious foci without limiting its effectiveness as the fundamental means by which we learn to live less anxiously and therefore more fully alive in the peace and joy of the present moment. Put another way, the daily practice of the Centering Prayer is not a mere meditational technique intended to jump-start or enliven the first twenty or thirty minutes of our day. Rather, "it is meant to open the way to living constantly out of the center, to living out of the fullness of who we are" (Pennington, 2001, p. 10). Anytime in meditational practice and/or in everyday life when we feel distracted or even hijacked by anxious thoughts and feelings and external circumstances, we can simply return to the sacred word or mantra that has the capacity to help us re-center in the gift of the present moment. And, if over time we connect the word or mantra to the rhythm of our breathing, it will become an even more powerful anchor and grounding force in the midst of the distracting mental chatter triggered by the exigencies of one's life. Interestingly, this parallels to some extent Ignatius' approach to contemplative prayer, specifically what he calls the "Third Method of Praying." In the Spiritual Exercises, he discusses the "Three Methods of Praying" that consist of (1) identifying the subject manner of contemplative prayer, e.g., "Our Father, in heaven" from the Lord's Prayer, (2) meditating on the deeper meaning of the particular mantra, and (3) repeating the sacred words "According to Rhythmic Measures" (Ignatius, 1991, pp. 178-182). Ignatius is of course referring to the rhythmic measures of our breathing, so that when we repeat the sacred mantra, one part of it, "Our Father," is said breathing in while the other part, "In heaven," is said breathing out. In the context of Centering Prayer, we could for twenty minutes repeat this mantra in rhythmic measure with our breath, breathing in "Our Father," breathing out "In heaven." For me personally, I could as I sometimes do take the mantra of the Franciscan prayer and repeat it for twenty minutes according to the rhythm of my breath, breathing in "O my God," breathing out "You are here," breathing in "O my God," breathing out "I am here," breathing in "O my God," breathing out "We are here…" In many ways, Ignatius' approach to contemplative prayer and meditation seems ahead of its time, particularly the Third Method of Praying, which almost seems to meld the Centering-Prayer method with the Zen breathing technique for meditation. Alternatively, I find it helpful to be mindful of the powerful double meaning of the Hebrew word *ruach*, repeating in my daily meditation or anytime throughout the day in rhythmic measure, "Breath" as I breathe in, "Spirit" as I breathe out.

For pastoral and spiritual caregivers, it is even worth incorporating other mindfulness meditation techniques and practices from outside the Judeo-Christian faith tradition. For example, certain Buddhist meditational practices put forward by Thich Nhat Hanh parallel Ignatius' Third Method of Praying, in that a sacred word or mantra can be repeated in rhythmic measure to the breath. One of these I use in my daily spiritual practice as well as anytime I am not focused on the gift of the present moment, either regretting the past or worrying about the future, is a simple yet deeply meaningful mantra from Hanh: Breathing in, "Present moment," breathing out, "Wonderful moment," breathing in, "Present moment," breathing out, "Most wonderful moment" (2006, p. 122). At times I have repeated this while walking the labyrinth, and find it to be a very helpful means of re-centering in present-moment experience, in the fullness of life, and in God's abiding love and presence. From the perspective of neuroscience, to pray or meditate rhythmically "in such a manner that one word of the prayer is said between one breath and another" (Ignatius, 1991, p. 181), will help us over time to calm the fear and stress regions of the brain while simultaneously building up higher-order structures in the prefrontal cortex. And, it is certainly worth incorporating other meditational approaches in our daily spiritual practice, even some that are more involved whenever we have the requisite additional time. Below is an example of a longer guided meditation that if done regularly in full or in part has the capacity to increase our level of compassionate awareness. We can have the meditation read to us by another person, as Hanson does for example with a recording of it. Or, we can read it to ourselves, in intervals, pausing in silence between lines. As I have discovered, after a while it is committed to memory so that I do not even have to open my eyes to read it. I try to use the following meditation on loving-kindness, in guided measure with my breathing, when I am feeling critical and judgmental of others and myself:

> Find a posture that helps you remain relaxed and alert. Settle into the breath…
>
> Be aware of the sensations of the breath in the region of the heart. Bring to mind the feelings of being with someone you love.

Keep feeling that love. Sense that love flowing through your heart, perhaps in a rhythm with the breath. Feel how that love has a life of its own, flowing through your heart, not specific to any one person.

Sense your love toward the people you know well, your friends and family. Feel a generous loving-kindness flowing through your heart in rhythm with the breath.

Feel that loving-kindness extending farther outward, toward the many people you know who are neutral to you. Wish them the best, too. Wish that they suffer less, that they be truly happy.

You may sense this loving-kindness like a warmth or light. Or like a spreading pool, with gentle waves extending farther and farther to include ever more people.

Feel your loving-kindness reaching out to include even difficult people; your loving-kindness has a life and strength of its own. Your loving-kindness understands that many factors affected these difficult people and led them to be a problem for you. You wish that even people who have mistreated you may suffer less. That they, too, may be truly happy.

The peacefulness and strength of this loving-kindness flows outward ever farther to include people who you know exist, though you do not know them personally. Sense loving-kindness for all the people living in your country today, whether you agree with them or not, whether you like them or not... (Hanson, 2009, pp. 171–172).

Chapter Five

A Therapeutic Framework for Neuroplasticity

The wise man is as a guest-house, and he admits all the thoughts that occur to him, whether of joy or of sorrow, with the same welcome, knowing that, like Abraham, he may entertain angels unawares...Let grief as well as joy lodge in the heart, for grief is sent for our benefit as well as joy. —Rumi, *Masnavi-i Ma'navi*

Early on a December morning in 1996, the neuroanatomist Jill Bolte Taylor at the age of thirty-seven experienced a massive stroke in the left hemisphere of her brain. Chronicling her experience in the best-selling book, *My Stroke of Insight*, she notes that the day began like any other day: the 7:00 a.m. alarm, getting out of bed, a brief workout on an exercise machine followed by a shower. But on this morning she did not feel like herself, as she was overcome by a sharp and throbbing pain behind her left eye combined with decreasing muscular coordination and garbled speech. An expert on brain science, Taylor had the knowledge not to mention the self-awareness to sense that there was a real "possibility that I was perhaps having a major neurological malfunction that was life threatening" (Bolte Taylor, 2009, p. 40). The coming days and weeks would indeed confirm that she had experienced a major malfunction in the brain, that she would need surgery to remove a blood clot that had triggered the hemorrhagic stroke. Taylor would spend the next eight years committed to the hard work of recovering all her functioning and cognitive ability, along with taking an "unexpected journey into the depths of my brain" (Bolte Taylor, 2009, p. 131). What she has learned from and through this journey of healing and recovery is that she and all other human beings are not simply a product of the brain. Instead, and this is something that she knows firsthand because she has studied *and* lived it, we have the ability if we so choose to regulate the cognitive loops of fear, worry, and anxiety that immediately follow a surge of feeling or emotion. Taylor has put forward what has become known as the "90-second rule," which means that, biochemically, the initial surge of any emotion only lasts for 90 seconds. It is quite remarkable for a brain researcher to intimate that before her recovery from the stroke no one had told her "that it only took 90 seconds for my biochemistry to capture, and then release me" (Bolte Taylor, 2009, p. 172). She uses the example of a surge of anger, which of course applies to a whole range of emotions, including for the purposes of this study the emotions of fear and anxiety:

> Once triggered, the chemical released by my brain surges through my body and I have a physiological experience. Within 90 seconds from the initial trigger, the chemical component of my anger has completely dissipated from my blood and my automatic response is over. If, however, I remain angry after those 90 seconds have passed, then it is because I have *chosen* to let the circuit continue to run. Moment by moment, I make the choice to either hook into my neurocircuitry or move back into the present moment, allowing that reaction to melt away as fleeting physiology....What most of us do not realize is that we are unconsciously making choices about how we respond all the time. It is so easy to get caught up in the wiring of our pre-programmed reactivity (limbic system) that we live our lives cruising along on automatic pilot. I have learned that the more attention my higher cortical cells pay to what is going on inside my limbic system, the more say I have about what I am thinking and feeling. By paying attention to the choices my automatic circuitry is making, I own my power and make more choices consciously. In the long run, I take responsibility for what I attract into my life (2009, pp. 146–147).

The 90-second rule is a remarkable finding and further highlights the promise and reality of neuroplasticity. Taylor's emphasis on directing the attention of higher-order cortical areas of the brain toward the automatic-pilot reactivity of limbic areas parallels what other researchers have described as the importance of developing the perspective of a third-party observer to monitor and modulate the contents of the mind. Or, as Siegel would say, it is harnessing the power of mindful awareness and observation in order to calm the mind's stormy activity, "to enable people to decouple automatic mental processes, such as flashbacks or intrusive memories, as well as habits of mind, such as derogatory internal voices or emotional reactivity" (2007, p. 279). We cannot of course control the initial trigger, for example, an anxious feeling or a painful memory, but after only 90 seconds the biochemical component of the emotional surge dissipates, giving us the opportunity to step outside of the neurocircuitry that would keep the anxiety, pain, and negativity alive and ever present way beyond its actual life. As pastoral and spiritual caregivers know all too well, the painful thought or anxious feeling can be kept alive for quite a long time, sometimes for a lifetime as the habitual and repetitive loops of worry and rumination feed and reinforce the neural pathways of negativity. It is important that practitioners, informed by neuroscientific research, develop an appropriate and relevant therapeutic framework to help those in our care find effective ways to "step out" of these repetitive loops, by learning to use the mind to rewire the brain. In so doing, we help our clients and congregants find ways to "consistently and persistently *tend the garden of the mind* moment by moment, and be willing to make the decision a thousand times a day" (Bolte Taylor, 2009, p. 154). Perhaps "a thousand times a day" is a bit hyperbolic, perhaps not in light of what we are learning about the brain's built-in predisposition toward negativity and anxious awareness. As the "shelf life" of a negative thought or anxious feeling is only 90 seconds, we discover, as Taylor has observed autobiographically, that "the more aware I remain about what my brain is saying and how these thoughts feel inside my body, the more I own my power in choosing what I want to spend my time thinking about and how I want to feel." She adds, and I choose to quote her at length because the words below have important and timely therapeutic implications:

> These passionate thoughts and feelings have the potential to jump instantly into my mind, but again, after their 90 seconds have come and gone I have the power to consciously choose which emotional and physiological loops I want to hook into. I believe it is vital to our health that we pay very close attention to how much time we spend hooked into the circuitry of anger, or the depths of despair. Getting caught up in these emotionally charged loops for long periods of time can have devastating consequences on our physical and mental well-being because of the power they have over our emotional and physiological circuitry. However, with that said, it is equally important that we honor these emotions when they surge through us. When I am moved by my automatic circuitry, I thank my cells for their capacity to experience that emotion, and then I make the choice to return my thoughts to the present moment. Finding the balance between *observing* our circuitry and *engaging* with our circuitry is essential for our healing. Although I celebrate my brain's ability to experience all of my emotions, I am cautious about how long I remain hooked into running any particular loop. The healthiest way I know how to move through an emotion effectively is to surrender completely to that emotion when its loop of physiology comes over me. I simply resign to the loop and let it run its course for 90 seconds. Just like children, emotions heal when they are heard and validated. Over time, the intensity and frequency of these circuits usually abate.... Paying attention to which array of circuits we are concurrently running provides us with tremendous insight into how our minds are fundamentally wired, and consequentially, how we can more effectively tend our garden (2009, pp. 154–156).

MINDFULNESS- AND ACCEPTANCE-BASED THERAPEUTIC
APPROACHES

Thus far we have noted breakthrough findings in the field of neuroscience, namely, the discovery that the brain is built for change via the process of neuroplasticity. "This is amazing because it demonstrates that we have the power to consciously change our brains and improve our neural functioning, in far less time than scientists use to think" (Newberg, 2009, p. 29). At the same time, we have also seen that the brain comes equipped with a built-in bias toward negative and anxious awareness, which can be if we are not careful reinforced by the theological constructs we apply in the work of pastoral and spiritual care. To confess that we are innately flawed and sinful, even if this is "theologically true," still reinforces the brain's predisposition toward negativity, triggering a confirmation bias that runs very deep in the limbic system. But as we begin to harness the power of mindful awareness through daily contemplative-meditational practice, we discover that we are not simply the product of our brain, nor are we completely powerless in the face of the 90-second upsurges of feeling and emotion. By mindfully and contemplatively tending the garden of the mind, we learn how to let a negative thought, an anxious feeling, and/or a painful memory come and go like a cloud passing through the daytime sky or a shooting star lighting up and almost immediately fading from the nighttime sky. Moreover, as we learn to observe the contents of the mind without getting hooked or hijacked by any of them, we open our de-cluttered hearts and minds more fully to the peace and joy of God's presence. Put another way, by following the 90-second-rule, we can reduce the hyperactivity of the mind in a way that keeps us more emotionally grounded and spiritually centered in the present moment, feeling less anxious and overwhelmed about tomorrow and the future.

Once again, this has important implications for the practice of pastoral and spiritual care, as more and more we find ourselves working with anxious clients and congregants. But apart from modifying our theology of original sin and encouraging those in our care to develop a daily spiritual practice, how do we go about caring for the anxious in a way that is most therapeutically effective and beneficial? Are there, for example, therapeutic approaches that align themselves more than others with the findings of neuroscience, in particular the discovery that the God-given brain is built for change? In the coming years, as Eric Kandel has observed, "using brain imaging to evaluate the outcome of different forms of psychotherapy" will become more commonplace, further clarifying that different therapeutic approaches "lead to different structural changes in the brain, just as other forms of learning do" (2006, p. 370). While many of us are familiar with the more traditional approaches to psychotherapy and pastoral counseling, e.g., psychodynamic, family systems, cognitive-behavioral (CBT), and so on, fewer of us have an understanding of more recent therapeutic modalities that intentionally build on the data emerging from neuroscientific studies and research. Known as mindfulness-based and acceptance-based therapies, these approaches to psychotherapeutic treatment have a certain affinity with cognitive-behavioral therapy in that they too focus on the cognitions and thinking patterns of a client. However, rather than focusing, like CBT, on the veracity of the thoughts and attitudes and their level of distortion, mindfulness- and acceptance-based therapies approach negative thoughts and anxious feelings as "transient reactions to different experiences, and the attempt to change their form or frequency is assumed to be a form of experiential avoidance" (Roemer & Orsillo, 2009, p. 202). Thus, while the focus of CBT is more on the cognitions and thoughts themselves, mindfulness- and acceptance-based therapies, informed by the findings of neuroscience, are more interested in how clients *relate* to the totality of their experience, including any anxious thoughts and feelings. "This involves moving from a focus on content to a focus on process—away from cognitive therapy's emphasis on changing the content of negative thinking toward attending to the way all experience is processed" (Segal *et al.*, 2013, p. 74). The *relationship* to the totality of one's experience becomes the focal point, particularly the extent to which clients can develop the necessary mindful awareness and observational distance needed for calming and regulating the mind.

How a client relates to the contents of his or her mind is central to the work of mindfulness- and acceptance-based therapies. Recall the acronym of COAL put forward by Daniel Siegel, which has to do with developing a curious and open and accepting stance toward our thoughts and feelings rather than one that is closed and avoidant. Cultivating an accepting, non-judgmental, and nonreactive awareness of our internal experiences calms the limbic areas of the brain, in particular the amygdala, which creates the neural space where neuroplasticity can occur. In this context, *acceptance* "refers to allowing what is to be rather than wishing or attempting to make it otherwise, but it does not necessarily mean liking things as they are" (Roemer & Orsillo, 2009, p. 115). What is most important is that the client develop an openness toward the full range of internal experiences, including as we would expect those that are positive and pleasant and, perhaps somewhat counterintuitive for those in our care, those that are unpleasant and sometimes even painful. For clients and congregants in the Judeo-Christian faith tradition, however, where one of the cornerstone theological constructs has been our original and inherent sinfulness, this could feel rather uncomfortable if not dangerous at first because of the assumption that God wants us to be pure and holy. While holiness is of course a desirable quality, it is never attained through the repression of our anxious thoughts and feelings, by keeping, so to speak, the lid on them. Jesus did not say that avoiding or repressing the truth about ourselves will set us free; rather, it is the quite the opposite of this: *knowing* the truth is what liberates us. As Freud discovered well before the emergence of modern neuroscience, the repressed thought or feeling or fantasy will always return again and again, only with greater force and power. In neuroscientific terms, as we learned earlier, reacting defensively, critically, and repressively toward our internal experiences only serves to stimulate the amygdala and the subsequent release of stress-provoking neurochemicals. With those in our care, we see again and again that fervent attempts to control and eliminate negative thoughts and anxious feelings does not result in a reduction of distress, but rather and perhaps paradoxically its amplification. Thus, while a more open, accepting, and present-moment relationship with the contents of the mind will not eliminate the distress triggered by an unpleasant thought or feeling, it will in fact help to "reduce the amplification that results from judgment, reactivity, and efforts at control," which in turn helps to "clarify internal experiences so that they can be normalized, tolerated, and potentially used more adaptively" (Roemer *et al.*, 2006, pp. 54 & 56).

For practitioners of mindfulness- and acceptance-based therapeutic approaches, what clients come to learn from the therapy "is not to change their thoughts, but rather to change their relationship to their thoughts, as well as their relationship to their feelings and sensations" (Segal, 2011, p. 110). This again represents a departure from a traditional CBT approach that focuses more on helping clients to determine the veracity of their thinking by distinguishing rational thoughts and attitudes from those that are irrational and less grounded in reality. Obviously, there are many clinical similarities with CBT, as we will see shortly when we turn our attention to the specific modalities of *mindfulness-based cognitive therapy* (MBCT) and *acceptance and commitment therapy* (ACT). For some neuroscientists, such as Richard Davidson, the combination of a mindfulness-based therapeutic approach with CBT holds great promise for initially creating a "neurally inspired behavioral therapy" and ultimately "neurally inspired therapy of all kinds" (2012, p. 153). Still, what sets mindfulness approaches to psychotherapy and counseling apart from traditional CBT approaches is first and foremost the emphasis on *acceptance*, specifically, "a recognition that thoughts, feelings, and sensations will inevitably arise (and inevitably fall) and that judging, fighting, or avoiding them is not very useful" (Roemer & Orsillo, 2009, p. 115). Indeed, judging, fighting, and/or avoiding our thoughts and feelings causes needless suffering, and illustrates the fundamental and noble truths of Buddhism: we suffer because we attach ourselves to the expectation that we are to be free of painful experiences, and are liberated when we let go of this illusion and accept life as it is rather than as we think it should be. Put another way, "acceptance is actively entering into the reality of what is rather than attaching to how we wish it to be or how much we like the way it is" (Roemer & Orsillo, 2009, p. 116).

Before turning our attention to the specifics of the MBCT and ACT approaches to therapy, it is important by way of further introduction to highlight several themes and therapeutic goals common to both as well as to other mindfulness- and acceptance-based therapies. First, clinical problems are seen as stemming not so much from the problems or difficulties themselves but more from the way the client *relates* to the internal contents of his or her mind. "This relationship can be 'fused,' entangled, or 'hooked' and is distinguished by an overidentification with one's thoughts, feelings, images, and sensations" (Roemer & Orsillo, 2009, p. 18). A client who refers to herself as an "anxious person" or another client who describes himself as a "depressed person" is repeatedly getting hooked or "hijacked" by negative thoughts and feelings, which in turn creates a fusion or overidentification with one's internal experience. Second, in an effort to escape or at least minimize distressing thoughts and feelings, clients will engage in "*experiential avoidance*," emotional, cognitive, and behavioral maneuvers intended to improve one's life that paradoxically lead to even greater distress and diminished quality of life (Roemer & Orsillo, 2009, p. 18). A client who engages in obsessive-compulsive thinking and behavioral patterns in order to suppress anxious thoughts and feelings and/or to preemptively escape potentially stressful situations in her life is presenting experiential avoidance, which as we learned from Taylor's research actually keeps the distressing thought or feeling alive long after its biochemical dissipation in the bloodstream. Third, the inability to relate openly to the contents of the mind, compounded by emotional and behavioral avoidance, leads to what is called a "*values-behavior discrepancy*" (Hayes *et al.*, 2012, p. 309), "which occurs when individuals who are struggling with internal experiences fail to engage in actions consistent with what matters most to them, further perpetuating their distress and dissatisfaction" (Roemer & Orsillo, 2009, p. 18). For example, a client who values and even longs for the care and support of a circle of friends, and yet frequently works late to avoid meeting with them because of persistent fears that he cannot be himself and/or that he must "put on a happy face" or be rejected because he does not meet their standards, is engaging in actions and behaviors that do not reflect his core values and what matters most to him.

The therapeutic goals for mindfulness- and acceptance-based treatment approaches correspond to the three foci listed above: "(1) alter individuals' relationships with their internal experiences, (2) reduce rigid experiential avoidance and increase flexibility and choice, and (3) increase action in valued directions" (Roemer & Orsillo, 2009, p. 31). Clients cultivate a mindful awareness of the totality of their internal experiences, learning to relate more curiously and openly and less avoidantly and reactively to transient thoughts and feelings that are like clouds in the sky or waves on the beach, here for a moment and gone the next, literally in 90 seconds if we simply let them be. Through a regular practice of mindfulness meditation and contemplative prayer, the behavior-values gap can begin to shrink until over time the client is living her life more consistently with her core values. As Siegel notes, "the general idea of the clinical benefit of mindfulness is that the acceptance of one's situation can alleviate the internal battle that may emerge when expectations of how life should be do not match how life is" (2007, p. 19). From the perspective of acceptance and commitment therapy (ACT), which we will explore in greater detail shortly, a mindful awareness and acceptance of the full range of one's internal experience is understood as

> *The voluntary adoption of an intentionally open, receptive, flexible, and non-judgmental posture with respect to moment-to-moment experience.* Acceptance is supported by a "willingness" to make contact with distressing private experiences or situations, events, or interactions that likely will trigger them. Acceptance should not be confused with self-absorption. An open posture to psychological experiences is not an end in itself. Psychological health is not attained by doing nothing but feeling one's feelings or sensing one's sensations from morning to night. It does not mean dropping everything and remembering in detail every memory that flits by in consciousness. Acceptance, as ACT practitioners mean it, has a *flexible* and *active* quality such that psychological events are noted and seen—even at times enhanced—moment to moment so that these events are available to participate in behaviorally if it makes sense to do so. Acceptance can sometimes have an unhealthy connotation. Indeed, the term is sometimes used as a kind of weapon against others ("You just have to grow up and accept it!"). Used in that way, *acceptance* means bucking up, tolerating, resigning oneself, or putting up with a situation—a passive form of acceptance does not necessarily predict positive health outcomes. *Acceptance* also does not mean wanting or liking something, wishing it were here, or judging it to be fair, right, or proper. It does not mean leaving changeable situations unchanged....It means to stand with your self psychologically and embrace what is present at the level of experience (Hayes *et al.*, 2012, pp. 272–273).

MINDFULNESS-BASED COGNITIVE THERAPY (MBCT)

Before offering two specific therapeutic modalities that build on mindfulness- and acceptance-based clinical practices, I want to be clear about my own therapeutic orientation. As a certified pastoral counselor and licensed mental health counselor, I purposely embrace a therapeutic style of practice that is eclectic, informed by a variety of different frameworks and modalities. I am therefore not a proponent of any one modality of therapy and counseling to the exclusion of all others. To be sure, more and more pastoral counselors and psychotherapists are embracing an eclectic approach to caregiving, for in reality there is something we can learn from the full range of therapeutic approaches. For example, I am not a psychoanalyst, even though I am informed by the Freudian and psychoanalytic understanding of unconscious processes as I go about the practice of pastoral care and counseling. Indeed, the repressed and unconscious contents of the psyche theorized by both Freud and Jung parallels in certain ways the findings of neuroscience, that the brain is predisposed toward negativity and avoidance. Nor do I exclusively embrace a family systems orientation, even though I am convinced that the individual client or congregant cannot be treated in isolation apart from a clear understanding of the relational systems that he or she inhabits: marital and romantic, family, community, cultural, congregational, and so forth. Additionally, while I am not a cognitive or cognitive-behavioral practitioner, I continue to be informed by CBT skills and techniques that promote new patterns of thinking and can therefore "alter brain activity in fundamental ways, enabling people to leave behind unhealthy patterns and go forward with new, healthier patterns that give them a renewed sense of joy and spare them the sadness, flat affect, and rumination that had proved so crippling" (Davidson, 2012, pp. 174–175).

In terms of my personal therapeutic "toolkit," which heretofore has included theoretical understandings and practical skills and techniques gleaned from psychodynamic, family systems, and cognitive-behavioral perspectives, I can now add the therapeutic perspectives of mindfulness-based cognitive therapy (MBCT) and acceptance and commitment therapy (ACT). While I continue to approach the work of pastoral care and counseling from the standpoint of an eclectic therapeutic orientation, and therefore do not see myself becoming an exclusive practitioner of MBCT or ACT, I do find myself incorporating more of the mindfulness- and acceptance-based theories and techniques into my practice as these therapeutic modalities more than any of the others intentionally align themselves with the important findings emerging from the world of neuroscience, particularly the discovery of neuroplasticity. In the words of Siegel, the mindful caregiver or practitioner can help clients and congregants cultivate a mindful awareness that enables them to "jettison judgment and develop more flexible feelings toward what before may have been mental events they tried to avoid, or towards which they had intense averse reactions" (2007, p. 278). In so doing, those in our care develop the capacity to take a "sacred pause" after the 90-second firing of an initial thought or feeling in order to step back and observe the habitual motion of their reactive neurocircuitry. Siegel further points out that "becoming nonreactive and developing equanimity in the face of stressors supports the view of mindfulness directly shaping the self-regulatory functions of the brain by promoting reflection of the mind" (2007, p. 278).

Mindfulness-based cognitive therapy (MBCT), as I have already pointed out, intentionally incorporates the findings of neuroscience into its approach to psychotherapeutic treatment. We have learned, for example, that cultivating a mindful awareness of the totality of one's internal experience initially requires a nonjudgmental stance, otherwise we set off a cascade of amygdala-hippocampus reactions in the limbic region of the brain. MBCT practitioners therefore begin by inviting those in their care to develop a stance of *welcoming* and *allowing* the full contents of the mind and internal experience, which simply means "allowing space for whatever is going on, rather than trying to create some other state" (Segal *et al.*, 2013, p. 276). To put it in the context of Siegel's COAL acronym, clients learn to develop a curious and open and accepting attitude toward their thoughts, feelings, and body sensations, including those that are easy and even pleasant to sit with and those that are not. Sometimes this will take some getting used to, as clients express initial incredulity at this rather "odd" and perhaps counterintuitive approach. I have even heard some of my clients express bewilderment, as they ask, "You want me to welcome my anxious thoughts and feelings?" or "You want me to allow my fears?" or even "You want me to be accepting of my panic?" The answer is most often "yes," but with some qualification: welcoming and allowing all of our internal experiences, including those that are difficult and painful, does not mean indefinitely, as if it will last forever. Nor does it mean even *wanting* or *liking* some of these experiences, particularly those that are painful. As Segal *et al.* put it in the important book, *Mindfulness-Based Cognitive Therapy for Depression*, "as we explore what happens when we step outside the struggle that arises out of 'not wanting,' little by little we are learning acceptance, how to relate differently to mental pain and anguish" (2013, p. 291). This *temporary* welcoming and allowing of all our thoughts and feelings puts an end to the fight or battle that goes on in the mind, which at bottom is really a fight we are having with ourselves. And this accomplishes very little except for firing up the limbic areas of the brain that keep us on edge and ever vigilant with and critical of ourselves. "Out of this new perspective we may see the mental pain change or dissolve by itself, revealing more clearly what action will be most helpful to take as a next step in dealing skillfully with our distress (Segal *et al.*, 2013, p. 291).

To reach this "new perspective" where we no longer fight with ourselves, or more specifically fight with or conversely indulge our anxious thoughts and feelings, requires the cultivation of the core skill of MBCT: *decentering*. We have already discovered that in order to harness the power of mindful awareness, it is necessary to develop an observational distance from and nonjudgmental meta-awareness of the contents of the mind, as if from the perspective of a neutral third party. In MBCT terms, this changed or decentered perspective "leads individuals to see their thoughts and feelings as mental events that come and go, that do not necessarily reflect important truths about their worth or adequacy as human beings, and that do not necessitate specific reactions or behaviors" (Coffman *et al.*, 2006, p. 34). This will naturally run counter to the brain's deeply ingrained predisposition toward negativity and anxious awareness, as we have learned, which assumes the need for a daily contemplative-meditational practice in order to keep in balance and even increase the neural positivity to negativity ratio. The vigilant awareness that at one time in our collective human history was exclusively directed outward toward the external world has more and more in recent times gone internal, as we automatically scan for any and all troubles lurking within the inner world of the heart and mind. Thus, for the MBCT practitioner, it is necessary to help clients *prepare* to decenter from the contents of the mind and to develop the necessary observational distance and meta-awareness, by way of the prerequisite skill of "attentional control." The main intention and rationale behind introducing the skill of attentional control is to prepare clients for the decentering process, which allows them to "step out of the 'automatic pilot' state of mind in order to nip in the bud the escalation of self-sustaining patterns of depressive thought" (Segal *et al.*, 2013, pp. 50-51). By extension, we can also include the self-sustaining patterns of hyper-vigilance and hyper-analysis that keep alive a negative thought or an anxious feeling well beyond its 90-second biochemical upsurge. In the context of MBCT practice, the fundamental skill of mindful awareness and attentional control

> is directly concerned with teaching people to decenter from their thoughts and emotions without avoiding, denying, or suppressing them. It teaches close observation of these phenomena and thus discourages experiential avoidance. It also teaches nonjudgmental acceptance and non-reactivity to these phenomena. According to the MBCT model, intentionally focusing undivided attention on thoughts, emotions, and sensations in this way uses much of the individual's capacity for attentional processing, so that little capacity remains for rumination (Coffman *et al.*, 2006, p. 34).

MBCT can trace its roots to Jon Kabat-Zinn's pioneering work in the area of mindfulness-based stress reduction (MBSR), which he began in 1979 at the Stress Reduction Clinic at the University of Massachusetts Medical School. Interestingly, both Kabat-Zinn and Zindal Segal, one of the founders of MBCT, were both contributors at the 2005 *Mind and Life Institute* conference that was referenced earlier in chapter two. Speaking at the 2005 conference, Kabat-Zinn pointed out that MBSR was designed to "create an environment where people can learn to slow down in their lives—or maybe even stop—and familiarize themselves with stilling the body, observing what is going on in both body and mind, and cultivating a certain kind of intimacy with the present moment as it is" (2011, p. 37). What he is describing is first and foremost *mindfulness*, the core skill of the MBSR medical program that has been linked, scientifically, to a reduction in stress, anxiety, and depression. Segal and his colleagues, after researching the MBSR program directly by way of field studies and research in the 1990s, developed the MBCT model of therapeutic treatment, which ultimately combines and integrates the mindfulness-based approach to stress reduction put forward by Kabat-Zinn with cognitive therapy. Echoing the words of Kabat-Zinn and therefore high-lighting the roots of MBCT in MBSR, Segal noted at the same conference that "the nature of mindfulness-based cognitive therapy is to help people become more aware, through systematic training in bringing their attention back to the present moment and looking at their experience from moment to moment rather than at what their minds tell them about the future or past" (2011, p. 107). Cultivating an intimacy with the present moment, by bringing our attention back to it again and again when we find our minds gravitating toward a painful memory from the past and/or a worry about the future, increases the mind's capacity for attentional processing so that little energy and focus remains for rumination and brooding. With the Sermon on the Mount in mind, we could say that cultivating an intimacy with the present moment increases the mind's capacity to be centered in the gift of *today*, so that there is less capacity for worrying and ruminating about *tomorrow*. As we become more mindfully aware of and grounded in the blessing of the present moment, we free the mind and brain, at least temporarily and even longer over time through the regular practice of contemplative meditation and prayer, from the repetitive cycles of excess negativity and vigilance.

The development and cultivation of a moment-to-moment mindful aware-ness has important implications for therapeutic practice in general and for mindfulness- and acceptance-based approaches in particular. In the context of MBCT practice, clients learn to "explore pleasant and unpleasant events from the same perspective, and they start to work with thoughts and feelings as mental events that are not necessarily true and need not be identified with strongly" (Segal *et al.*, 2011, p. 108). To help clients "decenter" from the assumed truth and factuality of their anxious thoughts and feelings, it is important to distinguish two very different modes of mind in the therapeutic treatment: doing and being. The former, the *doing* mode, is the mind left unattended on automatic pilot, characterized by old mental habits that "de-ceive us into attempting to 'think' our way out of our problems" (Segal *et al.*, 2013, p. 66). We can ruminate incessantly about how things *should* be differ-ent and better, how we ourselves should be more intelligent and successful, in better shape physically, calmer and less anxious, and so on ad infinitum. Once the "discrepancy monitor" is turned on in the mind, there is no stopping it from finding a solution to the perceived problem unless of course we develop the observational distance needed to harness the power of mindful awareness in the present moment. Problem-solving, as we all know, can be a good thing in the external world of human and social relations, but within the world of mental contents our attempts to solve the "problem" of feeling anxious, fearful, or unhappy by endlessly thinking and ruminating about it "can keep us locked into the state of mind from which we are doing our best to escape" (Segal *et al.*, 2013, p. 66). For many of us the doing mode will feel "normal," a natural state of mind if you will, but as we have seen throughout this study the endless attempts to think our way out of challenging circumstances and difficult states of mind will only amplify and reinforce the neurocircuitry that we are trying to control.

The doing mode of mind, which at times is a helpful ally in our lives as we deal with *solvable* problems, can work against us if we are not careful and mindfully aware of when it suddenly accelerates into a *driven-doing mode*. The result of this intensified form of doing mode is that the mind begins to continuously process more and more information, going round and round, dwelling on the discrepancies between how we want things to be and how they actually are in the present moment, both in the external world and within ourselves. In our daily spiritual practice, for example, "it is possible for one to try to mediate with so much focus on being someone who gets into a deeply relaxed state that if anything interrupts it, one feels angry and frustrated" (Segal *et al.*, 2013, p. 74). This is an example of meditating in a driven-doing mode rather than a *being mode* of meditational practice, which will defeat the centering purpose of contemplative spirituality because it ultimately stimulates the amygdala and the subsequent release of a surplus of stress-provoking neurochemicals. Whether we are engaged in meditational practice or any other daily pursuit, the fact is that "our continued dwelling on the way we are not as we would like to be just makes us feel worse, taking us even further from our desired goal" and confirming the fear that "we are not the kind of person we feel we need to be in order to be happy" (Segal *et al.*, 2013, p. 69). With a practical example from everyday life, Segal *et al.* illustrate that "the doing mode of mind can be really helpful—but often is not:"

> We can make clearer the distinction between helpful and unhelpful applications of doing mode by considering a simple task—driving across town to take part in a meeting. In the helpful version, the goal set is simply "be in the conference room of the Marshall Building by 2:00 P.M." Doing mode then devises a sequence of subgoals and actions to achieve that goal and puts them into action. If the action plan runs into problems, such as an unanticipated traffic jam because of an accident, then doing mode searches for alternative actions (find another route) and if none is available, accepts the inevitability of arriving late. We make our apologies, briefly consider ways we might avoid similar problems in the future, and that is that—no need to dwell further. In the driven-doing version, the self becomes entangled in the goal: "Be punctual at this meeting, as a conscientious person should be, so that others will respect you and value your contribution." ...When we get stuck in a traffic jam with this goal in mind, we add a further layer of "story" to our anticipation of arriving late: "I should have foreseen this. What will people think of me? We'll never get the contract now." We become anxious and agitated; we arrive at the meeting looking hot and bothered, with our minds more focused on our worries and concerns about others' judgments of us than on presenting a convincing argument. The meeting goes badly, we don't get the contract, and we come away dwelling on what a failure we are as a person. This is not

something that we can accept as easily as the simple fact "I arrived late," and
we spend hours ruminating on its implications…(2013, p. 70).

The goal of MBCT treatment is to help clients increase their mindful awareness so that they can begin shifting from a ruminative driven-doing mode of
mind to an alternative mode of mind, that of *being*. In being mode, "the focus
is on accepting and allowing whatever is present as it is, without any goal or
effort to change it" (Coffman *et al.*, 2006, p. 35). The contents of the mind,
therefore, such as negative thoughts and anxious feelings, are not viewed as
problems needing to be solved or fixed immediately, but are more helpfully
reframed as basic grist for the mill of human growth and development.
"Rather than thinking about problems or situations, *being* mode is characterized by direct observation and acceptance of whatever is happening in the
present moment—including thoughts and feelings that urge immediate action" (Coffman *et al.*, 2006, p. 35). Any compulsion to immediately act on an
anxious thought or feeling, the modus operandi of the driven-doing mode, is
simply viewed as the negativity bias of the brain prompting a hasty retreat
back into a more familiar, albeit more arrested, stasis and equilibrium. Again,
we do not have to want let alone like the particular thought or feeling or set
of circumstances of any given moment. However, our growth and development is dependent on increasing our capacity to embrace and live into the
"multidimensional complexity of experience," rather than reverting to the
"narrow, one-dimensional focus" of the doing mode (Segal *et al.*, 2013, p.
73). In doing mode, the mind continually travels back in time, scanning the
hippocampal memory bank for past solutions to problems and difficulties
that would appear to have a corresponding applicability to the present situation. Additionally, it travels forward to predict and preempt any future pain
and trouble by rehearsing solutions ahead of time. Indeed, the ruminative
focus of the doing mode on past and future uses so much of our attentional
processing that little capacity remains for being "here" in the present moment. "By contrast, in being mode, the mind has 'nothing to do, nowhere to
go,' and can focus fully on moment-by-moment experience, allowing us to
be fully present and aware of whatever is here, right now" (Segal *et al.*, 2013,
p. 72).

We can see that MBCT is not simply a solution-focused approached to
therapy and counseling, nor does it, like traditional cognitive therapy, focus
on affirming the rational thoughts and attitudes of a client while pointing out
those that are irrational. In the estimation of the MBCT practitioner, either of
these well-meaning approaches to therapy will unwittingly trigger the doing-
mode of mind that is fed by the brain's predisposition toward negativity and
anxious awareness. Nor, from the perspective of MBCT, does a focus on
problem-solving and weeding out irrational thoughts and attitudes lend itself
to cultivating an acceptance of and intimacy with the present moment, which

correlates with longer-term stress reduction. "The mindfulness-based approach does not just involve another, more clever problem-solving technique," but instead offers a different mode: "a way of 'being with' problems that allows people to let go of the need to solve them instantly" (Segal *et al.*, 2013, p. 179). Often, the client or congregant in our care will assume that discrepancy-based problem solving, the attempt to close the gap between how things should be and how they really are, is the royal road to increasing happiness and reducing unhappiness. "In this case, the 'gap' that needs to be closed is not a gap between our hand and an object, but between the *mood in which we find ourselves* and *the mood in which we want to be*." Segal *et al.* elaborate:

> The goal is clear: to escape or avoid unhappiness on the one hand, and to achieve happiness on the other. In order to see how successful we are at this, we need to monitor how we are getting on. Such constant monitoring of how we fare against the standards of happiness we have set for ourselves turns out to be very unhelpful. For example, to cope with waking in the morning feeling bad is difficult enough, but if we then match it against some standard, a better mood, we worsen the very mood we wanted to get rid of. Soon, we find that the results of this "matching" process create a new train of thought: "I wish I didn't feel this bad in the mornings. Why am I feeling this way? Why do I always feel this way?" (2013, p. 178).

With the findings of neuroscientific research in mind, MBCT practitioners are keenly aware that this doing mode, while feeling "normal" and intuitive to the client, merely serves to amplify and reinforce the neural predisposition toward hypervigilance and rumination. As we know from contemporary studies of the brain, the individual becomes trapped in a vicious cycle of neural reinforcement: the harder and more determined she tries to close the gap between feeling unhappy and wanting to feel happy, between feeling anxious and wanting not to feel anxious, the more powerful the neurocircuitry fueling the unhappiness becomes. "This 'not wanting' is like a locknut, holding in place a mode that is dominated by concept-based thinking—*thinking about* the feelings rather than directly experiencing them (Segal *et al.*, 2013, pp. 214 & 216). Shifting from a doing mode of mind toward a being mode of mind is central to mindfulness-based cognitive therapy. Clients are encouraged to leave the "battlefield" of the mind through decentering, to understand that fighting with our negative thoughts and anxious feelings, either indirectly through suppression and/or more directly and head on, will only leave us feeling more anxious. Segal *et al.* point out rather convincingly that "it may be a paradox, but if we cope with our unpleasant feelings by pushing them away or trying to control them, we actually end up maintaining them" (2013, p. 366). Even though it will initially feel counterintuitive to those in our care, in the long run cultivating an accepting and welcoming

scarcity

stance vis-à-vis the full range of internal experiences will calm the limbic structures of the brain, and this has the potential for keeping us more calmly grounded in the present moment. Acceptance, it bears repeating, is not synonymous with a passive resignation toward an anxious thought or feeling, nor is it necessarily wanting or liking it. "Quite the contrary: by accepting how we feel, we are just telling ourselves that this is our starting point," from which we can better decide what to do and how to act (Segal *et al.*, 2013, p. 366).

ACCEPTANCE AND COMMITMENT THERAPY (ACT)

In the final portion of this chapter, I will be presenting an overview of acceptance and commitment therapy (ACT), another therapeutic modality that is intentionally informed by the findings of neuroscience. Afterwards, pastoral and spiritual caregivers will have in their possession two neuroscientifically-informed therapeutic frameworks to situate their work with anxious congregants and clients. Like MBCT, ACT is also something of a counterintuitive approach that "goes against the grain of what most of us have learned needs to be done and ought to be done to alleviate human suffering, particularly in the West" (Eifert & Forsyth, 2005, p. 246). With the publication of the fifth edition of the *Diagnostic and Statistical Manual of Mental Disorders* (*DSM-V*), it is not difficult to see that the Western approach to mental health care is still very much influenced by and in the grip of the medical model of psychiatry, which tends to view psychological difficulties primarily through a *mental-illness* lens. Anxiety, for example, is pathologized as an abnormality and a classified disorder, and is therefore something that needs to be, in the course of clinical treatment, at least subdued if not eliminated. It stems from, in traditional psychodynamic terms, unresolved issues having to do with our early attachments to parents and caregivers, or, in CBT terms, it originates in our distorted and irrational thoughts and attitudes. Respectively, in the course of treatment, our anxious thoughts and feelings are either to be worked through cathartically in order to feel less burdened or reframed more logically and rationally. But this ultimately creates an internal struggle for the client: since the anxious thought or feeling is fundamentally part of her experience, the encouragement to work through and beyond it and/or to change and overcome it inadvertently reinforces the battle she is already having with herself. The ACT practitioner would encourage the same client to actively accept the totality of her experience, to let go of the internal conflict and battle and in doing so ultimately free herself from "the fundamental struggle and control agenda that many anxious clients are consumed with" (Eifert & Forsyth, 2005, pp. 69–70). And this is supported by the findings of neuroscience, for letting go of the battle within the mind has a calming effect on the limbic structures of the brain, in particular the amygdala. Thus, a fundamental goal of the ACT approach to therapy is "helping clients learn to accept themselves with all their flaws, weaknesses, strengths, and talents—the whole package" (Eifert & Forsyth, 2005, p. 70).

This does not mean that ACT embraces a naïve optimism, as if abnormal processes of psychological dysfunction or mental illnesses do no exist. However, while the ACT practitioner would acknowledge the pain of acute panic attacks or major depression, "the model underlying ACT holds that the ordinary processes embodied in self-reflective language and thought may actually *amplify* the core difficulties associated with such conditions" (Hayes *et al.*, 2012, p. 11). Here it is important to recall the famous Buddhist saying: In life pain is inevitable, but suffering is optional. In other words, "we suffer when we cling to or resist experience, when we want life to be different than it is," which always sets in motion in both the mind and brain "a waterfall of reactivity" (Brach, 2003, p. 106). Similarly, the ACT model distinguishes the inevitability and reality of painful experiences, both internal and external, from the suffering that comes later, a product of the mind's incessant analysis and commentary. It is not surprising, then, that one of the core foci of ACT is helping clients disentangle from the hyperactivity of this mental chatter, which parallels the MBCT focus on developing observational distance by way of decentering. "Suffering occurs when people so strongly believe the literal contents of their mind that they become *fused* with their cognitions" (Hayes *et al.*, 2012, p. 20), what the ACT therapist would describe as "cognitive fusion." As we learned from Jill Bolte Taylor's research and life experience, the fusion and therefore suffering can begin in as little as 90 seconds, once the physiological upsurge of fear or anxiety has dissipated. Hayes *et al.*, the founders of the ACT approach to counseling, illustrate the process of cognitive fusion by way of the following example from clinical practice:

> Suppose a client with panic disorder who is scheduled to give a presentation in a few weeks is becoming increasingly terrified. Suppose she or he imagines losing control while on stage in front of hundreds of people. In a fused state, this bad ending will seem immediately present and highly likely. The person may have fleeting images of going out of control or imagine the shock, horror, and derisive laughter her behavior would evoke in the audience. Anxiety is a natural response to the immediately present aversive events, and as these fused thoughts occur, the thought itself may occasion panic symptoms. This reaction in turn perpetuates the imagined embarrassment even further. The fearful person who constructs a fearful environment and then fuses with that thought acts as though the fearsomeness of the world has been discovered, not constructed... (2012, pp. 69-70).

Cognitive fusion, to one extent or another, is part and parcel of human life and experience, as it reflects the brain's predisposition toward keeping us out of harm's way at all costs. But as we are learning, this inherited predisposition toward vigilant awareness is often excessive and disproportionate for today's world, and therefore leads to no shortage of unnecessary suffering. The constant vigilance that was once directed outward toward the primal threats and dangers of the ice-age world, which was necessary for the individual and collective survival of human beings, is now often excessive for everyday life in *today's* world. We are still on the lookout for any sign of threat, danger, and/or confirmation that might reveal, for example, discord in our marriage, failure as a parent, the loss of a job, and so on. Additionally, the excessive vigilance is turned inward on ourselves, as we become fused with the voice of the inner judge or critic that incessantly reminds us of our flaws, weaknesses, and limitations as a human being. From the perspective of ACT, much of the suffering originates within these amygdala-driven processes that evolved to ensure our adaptability and survival as a species. This observation is the core idea behind ACT's *assumption of destructive normality,* "the idea that ordinary and even helpful human psychological processes can themselves lead to destructive and dysfunctional results, amplifying or exacerbating whatever abnormal physiological and psychological conditions may exist" (Hayes *et al.*, 2012, p. 13). When we become fused with or hooked by these "normal" cognitive and psychological processes, rather than observing them come and go from a position of decentered or, in ACT terms, *defused* meta-awareness, we increase the potential for greater suffering. This is a helpful reminder that "human suffering predominantly involves the misapplication of otherwise positive psychological processes of problem solving to normal instances of psychological pain" (Hayes *et al.*, 2012, pp. 18-19). Painful thoughts and anxious feelings will inevitably surface in everyone's mind from time to time, but instead of becoming cognitively fused with them as if they represent factual and literal reality we can develop the necessary mindful and observational distance to "watch" them come and go, as clouds in the sky or waves on the beach.

In the first part of this chapter, we learned that clients who define themselves as always being "anxious" (e.g., "I'm an anxious person"), or exclusively attached to any other emotional state, are overidentified and therefore fused with their thoughts and feelings. Cognitive fusion with the contents of the mind triggers the familiar cycle of suffering, which is then followed by another habitual process: *experiential avoidance.* "It is an immediate consequence of fusing with mental instructions that encourage the suppression, control, or elimination of experiences expected to be distressing" (Hayes *et al.*, 2012, p. 21). The initial cognitive fusion with an anxious thought or feeling, the fact that we have become "hooked" or "hijacked" by it, leads to avoidant strategies in the mind that are intended to head off a distressing experience from ever occurring or, if it has actually taken place before, from reoccurring again in the future. But experiential avoidance only makes the situation worse by reinforcing and keeping us hooked into the neurocircuitry of anxious awareness. "The long-term result is that the person's life space begins to shrink, avoided situations multiply and fester, avoided thoughts and feelings become more overwhelming, and the ability to get into the present moment and enjoy life gradually withers" (Hayes *et al.*, 2012, p. 22). Consequently, a central focus of the ACT treatment model is to help experientially avoidant clients engage more actively and less defensively with the fullness of life, including the full range of their internal experiences. For the ACT practitioner, "there are two main queries that typically 'feed' the ACT case formulation process: What kind of life does the client most deeply want to create and live? What are the psychological and/or environmental processes that have inhibited or interfered with pursuit of that kind of life?" (Hayes et al., 2012, pp. 105-106). The first query addresses the "commitment" dimension of ACT, while the second focuses on the experientially avoidant processes that hinder the "acceptance" of an authentic, meaningful, and in the language of the Sermon on the Mount, abundant life.

Pastoral and spiritual caregivers can certainly draw a parallel between the ACT approach to psychotherapy and the core of Jesus' gospel message, in that both focus on cultivating a meaningful and purposeful life. The ACT practitioner encourages individuals to live a life of authenticity and integrity consistent with their core beliefs and values, paralleling the words of Jesus that would encourage them to live more abundantly. In either case, we cannot live with abundance and authenticity if we are side-stepping or experientially avoiding certain aspects of our personal experience, for this stance toward life in general and toward our own personal lives will inevitably create a roadblock to a meaningful and valued life. This process of conscious and deliberate avoidance of painful thoughts and anxious feelings amplifies the suffering that we are trying to avoid, thus creating something of a Catch-22 situation. Interestingly, studies on thought suppression have consistently revealed that when individuals "are asked to suppress a thought or emotion, they subsequently show an increase in this suppressed thought or feeling as compared to those not given suppression instructions" (Hayes *et al.*, 2012, p. 75). Consciously and deliberately trying to suppress internal experiences, therefore, has the unintended consequence of further reinforcing the very thoughts and feelings that we are trying to avoid. It keeps us hooked into or fused with an anxious and fearful neurocircuitry that is amygdala-driven, making it much more difficult to feel fully alive and centered in the present moment. As Hayes *et al.* point out, "the act of running from scary feelings in the effort to feel more confident is not a confident action because that very act has no self-faith or self-fidelity" (2012, p. 76). Additionally, the act of running from our anxious thoughts and scary feelings exacerbates our personal suffering, which is something that *is* within our control to modify and reduce. Recall that pain, external and internal, is inevitable in life, something

that we cannot control, but suffering is optional and can be reduced the more
we harness the power of mindful awareness. The lessening of our own suffering, however, does not come as we might have expected through avoiding
and suppressing our anxious thoughts and feelings. Rather, the path toward
an abundant and valued life is through the *acceptance* of the totality of our
experience. For example, "when frightening feelings are present, the most
functionally confident action one can take is to feel them fully," which over
time reveals that "experiential acceptance is the *behavior* of confidence
(Hayes *et al.*, 2012, p. 76).

Obviously, experiential avoidance is deeply ingrained in the mind and
brain, a derivative of the ice-age brain that perpetually stands vigilant and on
guard to keep us safe at all times. The primal vigilance that was exclusively
directed outward at the grim realities of a very dangerous world has now
been redirected inward, focused more and more on the avoidance of potentially painful and threatening internal experiences. And, when the negativity
or avoidance bias of the brain is reinforced even more by certain cultural
biases and assumptions, the predisposition to avoid anything negative and
painful becomes even more pronounced. In the West, for example, we are
bombarded by a plethora of self-help literature and resources that convey to
us in no uncertain terms that we can and should feel good most of the time,
that we can and should *overcome* anything and everything painful and distressing by finding the right solution to the problem. "The ACT perspective,
however, is that the conceptualized outcome, that is, the supposed solution, is
often itself the problem" (Hayes *et al.*, 2012, p. 164). In this case, the solution seems rather intuitively and commonsensically to be the avoidance of
painful internal experiences. But avoiding and eradicating painful experiences is ultimately an illusion, a "rigged game" that "is made to seem win-
nable by the feel-good culture that promotes it" (Hayes *et al.*, 2012, p. 113).
In other words, while suffering is optional and therefore somewhat modifiable, pain is inevitable and unavoidable no matter how much Western culture
says otherwise. "When the client's behavior patterns are developed under the
aversive control contingencies that experiential avoidance entails, life becomes a game of avoiding personal experience, based on the belief that such
experience is toxic and poses a direct challenge to personal health" (Hayes *et
al.*, 2012, p. 113). Nor is the caregiver or therapist exempt from a similar
cultural biasing and conditioning, for we too are a product of the very same
cultural milieu. Thus, it is crucial for pastoral and spiritual practitioners to
maintain our own active meditational practice, so that the compassionate and
nonjudgmental awareness that we develop toward our own difficult and painful experiences can be extended empathically to those in our care. One of the
core competencies for the ACT model of care "emphasizes the importance of
therapists understanding that they are 'in the same boat' as their clients and

that they need to be willing to hold contradictory or difficult emotions without needing impulsively to resolve them" (Roemer & Orsillo, 2009, p. 71).

Our capacity to live more abundantly and therefore less anxiously is commensurate with our ability to experience life in all its depth and fullness, which we cannot do from a defensive and reactive position of avoiding our inner subjective world. Attempting to consciously and deliberately avoid and sidestep anxious thoughts and feelings only makes us more anxious and vigilant, for it keeps the limbic structures of the brain on constant and heightened alert. Moreover, the attention and focus we give to preemptively avoiding the experience of distressing thoughts and unpleasant feelings necessarily reduces our capacity for a more defused and spacious attentional processing, paralleling in certain ways the distinction MBCT would make between the reactive doing and the accepting being modes of mind, respectively. In the context of ACT therapy, clients begin to "examine the way that their desire to avoid experiencing negative internal experiences is at odds with their desire to live a fulfilling life" (Roemer & Orsillo, 2009, p. 95). The inability to accept the full range of our internal experiences, including those that are difficult and unpleasant, becomes a stumbling block to living a valued and abundant life, adding more suffering to the initial pain. This is the primary focus of the ACT model of treatment, to "address human concerns about anxiety and fear in a mindful, compassionate way, while encouraging people to pursue what really maters to them" (Eifert & Forsyth, 2005, p. 6). At bottom, its two major goals are "(1) fostering acceptance of unwanted thoughts and feelings whose occurrence or disappearance clients cannot control, and (2) commitment and action toward living a life that they value" (Eifert & Forsyth, 2005, p. 7).

In the course of the ACT therapy, clients see that their internal defensive strategies of "avoid and run," "search and destroy," and "control and eliminate" are counterproductive and at odds with the life they want to live. From the standpoint of MBCT, this would reflect a doing mode or even driven-doing mode of mind. Hayes *et al.* suggest that from a motivational perspective, it is important that the client grasp the considerable costs of continuing to follow these internally focused and unworkable change agendas, and the potential for spillover into other areas of his or her life:

> Control-and-eliminate strategies are by no means harmless—they materially worsen the client's situation. Not only is the client inadvertently producing more psychological pain, but also the persistence of control strategies almost inevitably seeps into the external world as well. This is so because one chief experiential avoidance strategy is situational or behavioral avoidance. Whenever clients begin to engage in situational avoidance, real-world consequences inevitably follow. The marital relationship suffers, work performance deteriorates, and health-protective behaviors (such as eating well, sleeping well, exercising) decline. Thus, the client is faced with the one-two punch of in-

creasingly uncontrollable psychological distress and the negative consequences of avoidant behavior in the real world (2012, pp. 167–168).

Chapter Six

Mindfulness and Acceptance Techniques and Practices

If I did not simply live from one moment to another, it would be impossible for me to be patient; but I only look at the present, I forget the past, and I take good care not to forestall the future. —St. Therese of Lisieux, *Story of a Soul*

In this last chapter I will be presenting case material illustrating interventions, techniques, and practices that reflect an informed understanding of the research and findings of neuroscience. Most of these derive from psychotherapeutic practice, in particular the mindfulness- and acceptance-based approaches to therapy and counseling that we were introduced to in the previous chapter. Practitioners of pastoral counseling and pastoral psychotherapy will find the techniques and practices clinically relevant and useful and can begin adding them immediately to their professional "toolkit." Pastoral and spiritual caregivers will also find the same techniques and practices helpful in framing their work with anxious congregants and clients, even if they do not have similar clinical training and expertise. As someone experienced in the various fields and disciplines of pastoral and spiritual care, pastoral counseling and psychotherapy, and mental health counseling, I would be the first to remind any pastoral or spiritual caregiver, as well as any other professional practitioner, to always work within and never beyond his or her scope of expertise and competence. That said, even in the more generalized fields of pastoral and spiritual care, it is important for practitioners to develop enough of a theoretical, methodological, and diagnostic framework in order to intervene effectively and skillfully with those in their care and to make the appropriate referrals when necessary. This presupposes at the very least a basic understanding of counseling theories and psychotherapeutic practices and techniques and how these can be applied to various psychological issues and disorders. Moreover, it is useful to have some understanding of empirical research and data that link certain counseling theories and practices to the effective treatment of specific psychological conditions, such as anxiety and depression. For example, after years of research and study it has become rather clear that the evidence-based treatment of choice for anxiety is cognitive-behavioral therapy (CBT), which is very important to know, conceptually and therapeutically, as we make our pastoral and clinical interventions. More recently, the findings of neuroscience have revealed specific ways to calm and soothe the anxious limbic regions of the brain, as we have been learning throughout this study, by way of mindfulness and contemplative-meditational practices. This information, too, is of fundamental importance to the work of pastoral and spiritual care, particularly at a time when clients and congregants are feeling more anxious about the present and future. In the remainder of this final chapter we turn our attention to specific case material that will highlight effective therapeutic techniques and practices informed by neuroscientific studies and research.

A MINDFUL AWARENESS OF THE PRESENT MOMENT

During his clinical training, Daniel Siegel worked with a twenty-six-year-old graduate student, Elaine, who was experiencing severe anxiety as she neared the end of her academic program. "She had been offered a job at a new company and felt terrified that she would 'fall flat' on her face if she accepted this challenging new position" (Siegel, 2007, p. 304). Siegel notes that by process of elimination, he ruled out the possibility of a medical and/or psychiatric condition, and thus proceeded to engage Elaine with conventional talk-therapy techniques. And yet, despite being a highly motivated client, she continued to be "stuck" in her anxiety and fear even after weeks of therapeutic treatment. At about the same time in his clinical residency, Siegel had begun to immerse himself in the neuroscience literature, particularly the "recently emerging findings about the role of the hippocampus in assembling pieces of implicit memory together into their explicit forms..." (2010, p. 89). Recall from chapter two that the hippocampus, located in the limbic region of the brain, weaves together the basic forms of emotional and perceptual memory into factual and autobiographical recollections. These hippocampal clusters of memory are reactivated all the time, often driven by an alert and watchful amygdala that biases the way we perceive and interact with the world around us. In anxious moments, the mind scours familiar memory banks of information, sorting and cross-referencing vast quantities of data, until it can find an explanatory match for the present situation at hand from the storehouse of neural memory clusters. Elaine's almost primal fear that she would "fall flat on her face" in this job opportunity intrigued Siegel;

perhaps her mind was sorting through memory clusters of earlier experiences, locating other moments in the past when she failed at a particular task or suffered something acutely painful and embarrassing.

Siegel was following his professional hunch that this troubled client, with so much promise and potential, was experiencing a reactivation of an earlier painful experience, driven and fueled by amygdala-hippocampus reactions. But as the therapeutic work was seemingly at a standstill, Siegel decided to introduce a reflective mindfulness exercise that would potentially help Elaine identify the contents of the mind that were getting in the way of her moving forward with her life. As he puts it, "I suggested that it might be helpful for her to get to know her own mind a little better" (2007, p. 305). As Elaine initially became more aware of her breath and body, she intimated to Siegel that she was feeling a painful sensation in her arm that extended up into her mouth and jaw. She began to cry, and Siegel asked her to describe what was being evoked. Elaine recalled that when she was three years old, she had fallen off of her new tricycle, breaking her arm and fracturing her front teeth. The accident twenty-three years earlier "had created an implicit mental model, or schema, coupling novelty and enthusiasm with intense fear and pain" (Siegel, 2011, p. 164). As she completed her graduate studies and pondered the exciting job opportunity, she was flooded by amygdala-hippocampus reactions and content streaming out of the limbic area of her brain. A deeply ingrained memory of another time and place when Elaine had literally fallen flat on her face was still, years later, holding her hostage to the fear that "trying new things could result in disaster" (Siegel, 2011, p. 164).

Siegel introduced a reflective mindfulness exercise that could help Elaine increase her conscious attention and awareness, both external and internal, offering a way forward out of the painful impasse. The exercise promotes a "simultaneity of conscious attention, in which you are focused both on the past and on your present-day self reexperiencing the past" (Siegel, 2011, p. 164). Both inside and outside the therapy sessions, Elaine would make use of the reflective mindfulness exercise that Siegel had offered to her, eventually making it a central component of her daily life. She would begin each day with ten or fifteen minutes of mindfulness meditation, and would find other moments throughout the day to meditate briefly, including during her lunch break at the new job she had decided to take after all. Siegel points out that this particular mindfulness exercise has become a starting point in his therapeutic practice with anxious clients, for it serves as an "anchor" to begin the day and return to as needed throughout the day, even in a briefer modified form. Below is an excerpt of the exercise that Siegel used with Elaine to help her get to know her mind a little better:

The mind is like the ocean. And deep in the ocean, beneath the surface, it's calm and clear. And no matter what the surface conditions are, whether it's

> *flat or choppy or even a full gale storm, deep in the ocean it's tranquil and serene. From the depth of the ocean you can look toward the surface and just notice the activity there, as in the mind, where from the depth of the mind you can look upward toward the waves, the brainwaves at the surface of your mind, where all that activity of mind, thoughts, feelings, sensations, and memories exist...*
>
> *At times it may be helpful to let your attention go back to the breath, and follow the breath to ground you in this deep tranquil place. From this depth of your mind, it's possible to become aware of the activities of the mind and to discern that those are not the totality of who you are, that you are more than just your thoughts, more than just a feeling. You can have those thoughts and feelings and also be able to just notice them with the wisdom that they are not your identity. They are a part of your mind's experience...just mental events that can gently float away and out of awareness* (2007, pp. 284–286).

Pastoral and spiritual caregivers can obviously modify this reflective exercise to fit their approach and professional style as well as the needs of particular clients and congregants. What is important is that the individual in our care be engaged in a regular practice beyond and between weekly appointments, otherwise the physiological, psychological, and spiritual benefits of meditational practices will be limited. While Elaine, for example, received quality care and guidance from Siegel in their sessions together, what was equally if not more important was what she was doing *between* the therapy sessions: daily meditation before she started work, a shorter meditation during her lunch break, and even brief re-centering moments of mindfulness breathing when at work she would feel anxious about "falling flat on her face." Thus, before clients and congregants can guide themselves through mindfulness and meditational exercises, they will often need the initial guidance and direction of the caregiver. Siegel notes that in terms of the reflective practice highlighted above, "people sometimes make a recording of my voice during this short, fifteen-minute meditation exercise" to use between therapy sessions (2007, p. 283). Remember that the mind and brain are not naturally predisposed to be calmly centered and at rest, so it will take some time before those in our care can self-direct themselves with a daily contemplative-meditational practice. We come into this world neurally hardwired for anxious awareness, constantly scanning both inner and outer worlds for any hint of threat or danger. Establishing a new baseline of functioning, a new "normal" as it were, will therefore require an investment of our time over the long term that reflects a way of life or being, rather than a quick-fix strategy. Through the daily practice of mindfulness meditation and contemplative prayer, there is the potential, *over time*, to rewire our brains in a way that the prefrontal cortical area, associated with higher-order executive functioning, can be further developed to better balance and calm the more anxious limbic structures. As Siegel has pointed out, neurons that fire together, wire together, so that the more we are firing prefrontal neurons in our daily contemplative-meditational practice, the more we are rewiring the brain to be at peace and rest in the present moment. "And so we can say that helping our clients, and ourselves, to practice mindfulness can be considered a form of brain fitness in that it stimulates the growth and presumably maintains the functioning of our integrative prefrontal circuits" (Siegel, 2010, pp. 180–181). In keeping our minds and brains healthy and "fit," we enter into a more patient and compassionate state with ourselves, others, the world, even God, knowing that ultimately "it takes effort and time to clear old structures and build new ones" (Hanson, 2009, p. 61).

This was true for "Pam," a woman in her sixties under the care of the Buddhist practitioner, Tara Brach. Pam, along with the help of hospice, was in the midst of caring for her terminally-ill husband, and in the remaining weeks of his life was feeling anxious and fearful that she was going to let him down by failing him. She intimated that "as far back as I can remember I've really been busy…But now…well, I just can't sit back and let him go without a fight" (Brach, 2012, p. 6). With certain parallels to Siegel's case of Elaine, Pam was also afraid of failure, in this case more terrified of "falling short" than of falling flat on her face. As far back as she could remember, Pam had lived her life in "overdrive," or in MBCT terms, driven-doing mode, a compensatory strategy to keep the fear of failure at bay and to keep from actually failing. She asked Brach if there was something more she should be doing for her husband, to comfort him and to ease his pain and suffering: "I'm afraid I'm going to fail at the thing that matters most," that soon "he'll die and I'll feel *really* alone, because I failed him" (2012, p. 6). Brach, a wise and skillful teacher and practitioner of mindfulness approaches and techniques, responded by conveying with empathy that the time for busyness and activity was over, that there was nothing more to *do*. Instead, Brach encouraged Pam to just *be* with her husband in the time he had left, to "let him know your love through the fullness of your presence" (Brach, 2012, p. 6). In the face of pain and loss, Pam's approach throughout her life was to get busy and become more active, externally and internally, what the MBCT practitioner would refer to as a doing mode of mind and the ACT practitioner would refer to as being experientially avoidant. Brach offered her another way to make the most of the time she had left with her husband, to embody loving presence simply by *being* that presence in the particular moment. "In the face of inevitable loss," Brach writes in *True Refuge*, and this has particular relevance for pastoral and spiritual practitioners, "this timeless presence brings healing and peace to our own hearts and to the hearts of others" (2012, p. 6).

But like Siegel's client, Elaine, Pam too was neurally hardwired to avoid the present moment, particularly those anxious moments when it felt like she would fall short and fail herself and others. To stay present with the totality of her experience, to simply *be* a loving and healing presence without need-

ing to *do* anything, would initially feel counterintuitive and therefore not
"normal" to this particular client. Just as Siegel had introduced a guided
mindfulness exercise and practice to Elaine, as a way of helping her become
more grounded in the present moment, Brach offered Pam a guided "presence meditation," which helps us relax our "armoring against the present
moment and allows us to meet life's challenges with a more open heart"
(Brach, 2012, p. 7). Pam, a practicing Roman Catholic, began to relax her
illusory grip of control, both inside and outside the therapy sessions, and in
so doing was able to be more accepting of her present-moment experience.
Moreover, she began to experience her religious faith more deeply as a
dynamic resource with the capacity to sustain her during this difficult time.
Still, in the face of her husband's final turn for the worse, Pam lamented that
"this shouldn't be happening—so much exhaustion, so much pain," that it is
just "plain wrong" for someone to be going through something like this
(Brach, 2012, p. 6). Brach invited her to simply *be* with and present to
whatever she was feeling, her fear and sadness and grief, and to inwardly
whisper the words, "I consent," again and again. "I had recently heard this
phrase from Fr. Thomas Keating," writes Brach, "and thought that as a
Catholic, Pam might find it particularly valuable" (2012, pp. 6–7). Indeed,
the "I consent" is central to Keating's method of Centering Prayer, a way of
reaffirming our intention to align ourselves more fully with God's presence
and action within. As Keating notes, "This renewal of the will's consent, as it
becomes habitual, creates an atmosphere in which you can simply pay little
or no attention to the normal and inevitable flow of thoughts" (2006, p. 22).
Increasingly, Pam was able to be more fully present with the totality of her
experience, with the gratitude she felt for the life she had shared with her
beloved husband, *and* with the deep grief and sadness in the face of his
declining health and impending death. Brach recalls the following exchange
with Pam, a month after her husband had died:

> "Over those last few weeks I had to keep letting go of all my ideas of how his
> dying should be and what else I should be doing, and just remind myself to
> say, 'I consent.' At first I was mechanically repeating the words, but after a
> few days I felt as if my heart actually started consenting." [Pam] described
> how she would pause when she was gripped by strong feelings and check
> inside to see what was going on. When her gut tightened with clutches of fear
> and feelings of helplessness, she would stay with those feelings, consenting to
> the depth of her vulnerability. When the restless urge to "do something" arose,
> she would notice that and be still, letting it come and go. And as the great
> waves of grief rolled through, she would again say, "I consent," opening
> herself to the huge aching weight of loss. This intimate presence with her inner
> experience allowed Pam to fully attend to [her husband] (2012, p. 9).

Brach reminds us that *presence* is not a grandiose or exotic state, nor is it something that we have to search for or manufacture for ourselves. In the simplest terms, presence "is the felt sense of wakefulness, openness, and tenderness that arises when we are fully here and now with our experience," and as such it is "immediate and embodied, perceived through the senses" (2012, p. 12). In mindfulness- and acceptance-based terms, presence represents a being rather than a doing mode of mind, an accepting rather than avoidant stance toward the totality of our experience. Below is the guided meditation that Brach introduced to Pam, as a way of helping her consent to the fullness of her present experience. Brach calls the meditation "A Pause for Presence," noting that "a natural entry into presence is through your body:"

> *Find a place to sit comfortably and close your eyes. Begin with three conscious breaths: Inhale long and deep, filling the lungs, then exhale slowly, sensing a letting go of any tensions in your body and mind.*
>
> *Invite your awareness to fill your whole body. Can you imagine your physical form as a field of sensations? Can you feel the movement and quality of the sensations—tingling, vibrating, heat or cool, hard or soft, tight or flowing? Take a few moments to bring your full attention to this dance of sensations.*
>
> *Now let your awareness open out into the space around you. Can you imagine receiving the symphony of sounds, letting it wash through you? Can you listen to the changing play of sounds, not just with your ears but with your whole awareness? Take a few moments to bring an open attention to listening to sounds.*
>
> *Keeping your eyes closed, let your awareness receive the play of images and light at the eyelids. You might notice a flickering of light and dark or certain shapes, shadows, or figures of light. Take a few moments to attend to seeing.*
>
> *Feeling your breath and sensing the space around you, be receptive to any scents that might be in the air. Discover what it is like to smell and receive the odors present in the surrounding area.*
>
> *Now let all your senses be wide open, your body and mind relaxed and receptive. Allow life to flow freely through you. Take as long as you'd like, listening to and feeling your moment-to-moment experience. Notice the changing flow of sensations, sounds, aliveness, and also the background of presence that is here. Let yourself appreciate this awake, inner space of presence. When you are finished, sense the possibility of bringing an alert, open awareness to whatever you are doing next.*
>
> *As you move through the day, pause periodically and briefly reawaken your senses, primarily by feeling bodily sensations and listening to sounds. With practice, you will become increasingly at home in natural presence* (2012, p. 15).

PRACTICAL METHODS FOR TRAINING THE MIND

It is important to recall that the practice of mindfulness meditation and con-templative prayer is not a form of escapism from the realities of life and the world. Developing the capacity to harness the power of mindful awareness through daily spiritual practice helps us rewire the mind and brain in a way that we are more directly engaged with the fullness of life and less prone to living reactively on automatic-pilot. For Christians, it is reminiscent of the example put forward by Jesus, who after extending himself ministerially through preaching, teaching, healing, and caring for the poor, would out of necessity "go away" again and again in order to recenter himself for the demands of the coming days. A daily practice of contemplative prayer and meditation is therefore not intended as a self-indulgent exercise, nor is it meant as an escape, even temporary, from the difficulties and practicalities of life. Instead, "what is produced is a more enduring sense of well-being that goes beyond a short-lived positive feeling" (Altman, 2010, p. 28), guiding us toward a deeper and more meaningful engagement with the fullness of life. The assumption that contemplative spiritual practice is at best optional for the person of faith or at worst a distraction from "real life" is unfortunate, for what we are learning from neuroscience is that through daily mindfulness and meditational practices we can literally rewire the brain in order to keep us more grounded in the present moment of lived experience. Said another way, the findings of neuroscience are revealing that with a regular contem-plative-meditational practice, it is possible to foster neuroplasticity and by extension an increase in positive and lasting feelings of peace, kindness, and compassion for ourselves and for others. "Methods of training the mind for compassion and peace offer the hope that life can be experienced in a vastly more loving and caring way than it usually is on our blue planet" (Altman, 2010, p. 29).

The resistance that we sometimes feel to developing a daily spiritual practice, even for those of us in religious faith communities, can be, as Lizabeth Roemer and Susan Orsillo point out, a form of experiential avoid-ance. Contemplative prayer and meditation, to be sure, is not always easy nor is it always relaxing, for at one time or another a painful thought or feeling will inevitably arise in the panorama of our awareness. Thus, clients and congregants "may find the thoughts and feelings that arise during practice and during their daily lives upsetting and look for reasons to avoid practice and awareness" (Roemer & Orsillo, 2009, p. 134). A fairly common reason or more accurately rationalization for avoiding regular meditational practice, which caregivers and clinical practitioners will frequently hear, is that it takes too much time. To state the obvious, we are a busy and hurried culture of immediacy and immediate gratification, so this can give the individual a needed alibi to rationalize his or her avoidance. Roemer and Orsillo note that caregivers can respond empathically to any manifestation of avoidance, conveying for example that it does in fact take time and patience to develop a daily mindfulness and meditational practice: "If it were easy...we would all do it naturally, and clearly we do not" (2009, p. 134). They offer the following case vignette to illustrate that "while validating doubts clients may have about the potential usefulness of this practice, therapists can ask them to commit to trying some of the prescribed exercises and watching to see whether or not they seem beneficial":

Client: I just couldn't set aside any time for the practice this week. I have too much else going on.
Therapist: I know how challenging it can be to find extra time. Can you give me an example of a particular day and what happened when you tried to practice [the meditation]?
Client: I thought I would wake up in the morning and do the breathing for a few minutes. ...But then I started thinking about everything I had to do that day, and I just didn't see how sitting and doing nothing would help at all. ...
Therapist: I really understand that reaction. ...In a way, I'm asking you if you can take a leap of faith and just do these practices, even if they feel like a waste of time, for a couple of weeks. ...What about trying to practice for only five minutes a day this coming week?
Client: Really? Is that enough time?
Therapist: It's much better to practice for five minutes regularly than to set your goals so high that you don't do it at all...
Client: I can definitely do five minutes.
Therapist: OK, remember you're still probably going to feel it's a waste of time. And you might still feel that after you practice. It might be boring or anxiety-provoking, or you might feel bad at it and think, "Why did she tell me to do this?" Do you think you can stick with it even if all of those things happen?
Client: Yeah, I can do anything for five minutes... (Roemer & Orsillo, 2009, pp. 134–135).

The therapeutic vignette illustrates that initially a daily meditational practice will not come easily and naturally for anyone, either for ourselves or for those in our care. As we have seen the mind and brain are more predisposed to *do* rather than *be*, so at first it may feel like we are unproductively wasting part of the day when so much needs to get done. The therapist in the vignette above effectively normalized the client's initial apprehension at the thought of committing to lengthy daily meditations, particularly when there is "too much else going on," offering instead a more modest proposal to help the person get started and become habituated to a rhythmic practice: five minutes at a time. While this is of practical value for the therapy, it also reflects an understanding of neuroscience on the part of the therapist. For hearing a client affirm more calmly and less agitatedly that "I can definitely do five minutes" corresponds to a downshifting in the limbic structures of the brain, most notably the amygdala. Segal *et al.*, in the context of MBCT, even offer a briefer meditational practice to new clients, what they call the "Three-Minute Breathing Space Meditation." This becomes "an important vehicle for bringing formal meditation practice into daily life," helping clients to see that "it is a way to pause, even in the midst of a hectic day, and reestablish contact with the present moment" (2013, p. 196). The following exchange between client and therapist highlights rather well the MBCT rationale for introducing new clients to meditational practice by way of a brief three-minute exercise:

Client: My attention wandered, not at the beginning, but about fifteen seconds after I was into it. And then I got it together again. Is that because you're aware that it's going to be short?
Therapist: It may be. The idea of being aware for a single breath seems doable; the idea of being aware of your breath for half an hour seems an enormous task. But in reality, you can simply take it breath by breath. It's like having an enormous pile of logs in front of you that you have to move. If you contemplate the whole pile, your heart sinks and your energy fails. But you know if you could just focus on the one you've got to do now, give your full attention to that, then take the next one, then it becomes doable (Segal *et al.*, 2013, p. 198).

The Three-Minute Breathing Space Meditation conveniently has three simple steps: (1) "Stepping out of automatic pilot to….recognize and acknowledge one's experience at the moment," (2) "Bringing the attention to the breath, gathering the scattered mind to focus on the single object—the breath," and (3) "Expand the attention to include a sense of the breath and the body as a whole" (Segal *et al.*, 2013, p. 196). Automatic pilot is of course the preferred state of the brain, at least the limbic region that is driving us to remain alert and vigilant lest we succumb to the dangers and threats in both external and internal worlds. But as we have learned, the surplus of amygdala-driven energy and reactivity is often excessive for the present moment and set of circumstances, and therefore requires an intentional "stepping out" in order to cultivate observational distance and mindful awareness. From the case examples described above, we can see that it does not take long in the context of mindfulness meditation for the amygdala to begin firing up, even after only fifteen seconds. It is simply doing its job of keeping us alert and vigilant for what might lie ahead throughout the day and in the days to come. In the earlier vignette, the thought crosses the client's mind that there is so much going on and therefore so much to do and not enough time to get it all done, and even less time if he or she is engaged in meditational practice, i.e., "sitting and doing nothing." This natural hypervigilance is hard to turn off initially, but over time and through regular meditational practice it becomes possible to tone it down enough to step out of the driven-doing mode of automatic pilot in order to cultivate a mindful awareness of the present moment. In MBCT, the client is encouraged to think in terms of initial small steps, three minutes of meditational practice that focuses on the breath and the body. The exercise could be modified for clients or congregants engaged in the Centering Prayer, as we will see shortly, helping those in our care to focus in three or five minutes on their sacred word or mantra.

For contemplative-meditational practice, the breath can be a useful anchor that stabilizes our awareness when we become flooded with, in the words of Thomas Keating, "the wanderings of the imagination." Recall that in chapter four we noted that the Hebrew word, *ruach*, has a double meaning: breath *and* spirit. The familiar saying, God is closer than our breath, now becomes even more relevant and meaningful, for the air that we breathe in and the Spirit we breathe out are simultaneously the ground of our being and the manifestation of divine presence. Thus, whether we are engaged in mindfulness meditation or contemplative Centering Prayer, the breath can be the stabilizing anchor that calls us back from the wanderings of the imagination, which as we know can begin even after a mere fifteen seconds. As Keating writes, "the imagination is a perpetual-motion faculty and is constantly grinding away," so clients and congregants, notably those individuals with perfectionist tendencies, will need to keep in mind that "it is unrealistic to aim at having no thoughts" (2006, p. 43). It is simply a matter of coming back to the breath, or in the context of Centering Prayer, returning to the sacred word or mantra. Keating suggests, as we learned earlier, twenty minutes as the ideal format for practicing the Centering Prayer, but there is nothing wrong with shortening the length of the prayer or meditation when we have less time. As with Elaine, the anxious graduate student in Siegel's care, the contemplative-meditational practices that we begin the day with are ours to use throughout the day, even in a shorter and modified form. The important thing is that we are doing it regularly enough to build up and increase prefrontal structures and functioning in the brain, whether this be for twenty or five or three minutes or any combination of these throughout the day.

Perhaps it is best for pastoral and spiritual caregivers, like the MBCT therapist with the breathing-space meditation, to also think shorter when first introducing the Centering Prayer to an anxious client or congregant. The idea of meditating on a sacred word or mantra initially for a few minutes will seem more doable for anxious individuals, whereas the idea of being centered in the word or mantra for twenty or thirty minutes will feel to some like yet another task to add to an ever growing list of "to-do's." But in reality, the client or congregant can take it breath by breath or mantra by mantra, recognizing that it is only a matter of time before the distracting wanderings of the imagination begin to fill the mind. For example, the anxious thought or feeling may have to do with everything else that is going on in our lives, as we saw in the earlier case vignette, and how little time there is to get it all done. Sometimes, though, we can experience in the midst of our meditational practice a breakthrough thought that seemingly helps us to see things in a more helpful and positive light. We may find ourselves wanting more to keep the thought alive than to focus on the stabilizing breath or sacred mantra, so we do not forget it afterwards. Keating, however, reminds us that our daily spiritual practice is "the time to let go of all thoughts, even the best of thoughts," for "if they are really good, they will come back later" (2006, p. 49). True, God can speak to us in many different ways, including at times through our thoughts and feelings, "but keep in mind that God's first language is silence" (Keating, 2006, p. 48).

In chapter four, we summarized the four steps of the Centering-Prayer method: (1) find a relaxing place where we can sit comfortably, (2) choose a word or mantra that becomes the sacred object of our attention for the twenty minutes or so of meditational time, (3) the sacred word or mantra symbolizes our intention to be fully present with God, and (4) when we become distracted by intruding thoughts and the wanderings of our imagination, we simply return gently to the word or mantra as that which keeps us anchored in God's loving presence. Keating's emphasis on resisting no thought, retaining no thought, and reacting emotionally to no thought demonstrates a keen awareness of neuroscientific findings, for doing the opposite of this (resisting, retaining, and reacting to the wanderings of the imagination) will only serve to fire up an already alert and watchful amygdala. A contemplative participant at the 2005 *Mind and Life Institute*, along with leading neuroscientists and the Dalai Lama, Keating is also conveying an awareness of and respect for mindfulness approaches, therapeutic, pastoral, and spiritual, which encourage clients to allow and accept the totality of internal experiences without avoiding or getting fused with them. As congregants and clients habituate themselves to the daily practice of Centering Prayer, they will sometimes discover that in the quiet of the meditational space they "may reach a place where the sacred word disappears altogether and there is an awareness of no thoughts" (Keating, 2006, p. 126). In neurological terms, this would reflect "the paradoxical phenomenon of focusing so intently on one's capacity to focus that focus itself dissolves" (Bulkeley, 2005b, p. 157). For Keating, this is a reflection of the "clear experience of interior silence," when we are truly "resting in God" and the knowledge of God's primary means of communication: silence. To facilitate this deeper experience of interior silence and resting in God's loving presence, Keating offers the following meditation:

We begin our prayer by disposing our body. Let it be relaxed and calm, but inwardly alert.

The root of prayer is interior silence. We may think of prayer as thoughts or feelings expressed in words. But this is only one expression. Deep prayer is the laying aside of thoughts. It is the opening of mind and heart, body and feelings—our whole being—to God, the Ultimate Mystery, beyond words, thoughts, and emotions. We do not resist them or suppress them. We accept them as they are and go beyond them, not by effort, but by letting them all go by. We open our awareness to the Ultimate Mystery whom we know by faith is within us, closer than breathing, closer than thinking, closer than choosing—closer than consciousness itself. The Ultimate Mystery is the ground in which our being is rooted, the Source from whom our life emerges at every moment.

We are totally present now with the whole of our being, in complete openness, in deep prayer. The past and future—time itself—are forgotten. We are here in the presence of the Ultimate Mystery. Like the air we breathe, this divine Presence is all around us and within us, distinct from us, but never separate from us. We may sense this Presence drawing us from within, us if touching our spirit and embracing it, or carrying us beyond ourselves into pure awareness.

We surrender to the attraction of interior silence, tranquility, and peace. We do not try to feel anything, reflect about anything. Without effort, without trying, we sink into this Presence, letting everything else go. Let love alone speak: the simple desire to be one with the Presence, to forget self, and to rest in the Ultimate Mystery.

This Presence is immense, yet so humble; awe-inspiring, yet so gentle; limitless, yet so intimate, tender and personal. I know that I am known. Everything in my life is transparent in this Presence. It knows everything about me— all my weaknesses, brokenness, sinfulness—and still loves me infinitely. This Presence is healing, strengthening, refreshing—just by its Presence. It is non-judgmental, self-giving, seeking no reward, boundless in compassion. It is like coming home to a place I should never have left, to an awareness that was somehow always there, but which I did not recognize. I cannot force this awareness, or bring it about. A door opens within me, but from the other side. I seem to have tasted before the mysterious sweetness of this enveloping, permeating Presence. It is both emptiness and fullness at once.

We wait patiently; in silence, openness, and quiet attentiveness; motion-less within and without. We surrender to the attraction to be still, to be loved, just to be (2006, pp. 129–130).

THE USE OF ACCEPTANCE-BASED METAPHORS

In the final part of this chapter, I will be presenting case material illustrating ACT techniques and therapeutic practices specifically designed for the anxious client. A central therapeutic strategy for the ACT practitioner, which is aimed at undermining cognitive fusion and the habitual avoidance of internal experiences, is the use of metaphors. Because they are nothing more than stories, and therefore cannot be taken literally, metaphors "allow clients to make experiential contact with an aspect of their experience that may be frightening for them to contact" (Eifert & Forsyth, 2005, p. 103). This helps clients create a certain space and distance between themselves and the ways they habitually respond and react to their anxious thoughts and feelings. In so doing, clients learn to take a "pause" in the face of difficult and unpleasant internal experiences, creating the observational distance necessary for cultivating greater mindful awareness and receptive attention. In certain ways, mindfulness- and acceptance-based approaches can be thought of as variations on "pause therapy" in that practitioners "help clients pause between their emotional reaction and their behavioral action so that their actions can be informed but not dictated by their emotional responses" (Roemer & Orsillo, 2009, p. 94). In physiological terms, the client begins to decouple automaticity in the brain by learning to disengage from amygdala-hippocampus reactions. In spiritual terms, this "sacred pause" creates the necessary space for the Holy Spirit or the Sacred Third to more fully fill our hearts and minds with the peace and joy of God's abiding presence. For the pastoral or spiritual caregiver guided by the ACT model, what can help foster the creation of a sacred pause and the building of sacred space is the application of relevant and useful metaphors. "Studies have shown that figurative metaphorical language is emotionally more meaningful, and hence more likely to impact a person's overt behavior, than straightforward rational-logical talk" (Eifert & Forsyth, 2005, p. 103).

Below are three specific metaphorical strategies that are intended to help anxious clients be more accepting and less avoidant of their internal experiences. So often the ways that clients have "attempted to manipulate thoughts and feelings (e.g., drugs, alcohol, overt avoidance, sex, attacking others, moving away, social withdrawal, and so on)," and therefore avoid certain areas of their personal experience, prove unworkable and counterproductive (Hayes *et al.*, 2012, p. 190). To help them see the ultimate futility of their previous efforts and the need for a more creative and effective solution, the therapist can introduce a metaphorical intervention designed "to help clients trust their own experience and begin to open up to a transformational alternative" (Hayes *et al.*, 2012, pp. 189–190). For example, the caregiver may decide to offer the following core ACT intervention, the *Person in a Hole* metaphor, which is designed to "let clients experience the hopelessness of their struggle with anxiety and that it may be time to adopt a fundamentally different strategy when anxiety shows up";

Caregiver: Imagine a [person] running through a wide-open field…and falling into a hole. It's a hole named anxiety. It wasn't the person's fault—it just happened.…The person struggles and struggles to climb out of the hole, but there is no escape. …All this effort and hard work. And what is the result? The hole has only gotten deeper and wider, and she is more scared and frustrated. Is this your experience? Clearly, the problem is not lack of effort. Just like the person who gave all she had to dig herself out, you've tried everything, too: you've used the distraction dig, the relaxation dig, the positive thinking dig, the seeing-a-therapist dig. Yet all this effort has not paid off.…The bottom line is, you're still digging, and that only gets you deeper into the hole.…Has it helped you when you listened to your mind and did all those things?

Client: Sometimes those things have worked a bit, but ultimately they have been pretty useless (Eifert & Forsyth, 2005, pp. 137–138).

Once the client feels less compelled to dig his or her way out of the anxiety hole, or in MBCT terms, to be less attached to the driven-doing mode of mind and more open to the being mode, the individual can then become more tolerant and even curious of the wider range of internal experiences as they are in the present moment rather than as they *should be*. With increasing observational distance and mindful awareness that correlates with a calming of the limbic region of the brain, clients can learn to "befriend" their anxious thoughts and feelings, which previously have held them hostage in a state of emotional and spiritual captivity. Here is where another core ACT intervention can be introduced as a follow-up to the previous metaphorical strategy, namely, the *Bus Driver* or the *Passengers on the Bus* metaphor. The client is pictured as the driver of the bus, and along the road "picks up a number of unruly bully passengers (anxiety-related thoughts and feelings) that yell at the client to change course and go where they want to go instead of where the client wants to go" (Eifert & Forsyth, 2005, p. 197). As Hayes *et al.* note, the bus-metaphor intervention aims at "deliteralizing provocative psychological content through objectification," allowing our anxious thoughts and feelings to become things or people (2012, p. 250). This makes them less emotionally threatening, giving clients the opportunity to extend the sacred pause and to widen their window of tolerance, thus regulating and stabilizing the activity of the mind. Physical metaphors, like the *Person in the Hole* and the *Bus Driver*, "can be used to accomplish this objectification to great effect, since we naturally see external objects and other people as separate from ourselves" (Hayes *et al.*, 2012, p. 250). Below is a case vignette illustrating the introduction of the bus exercise in a counseling session. "The basic idea is that clients can drive and act in a valued direction no matter what the anxious passengers throw at them and tell them to do," which translated means that they can "let values, not their anxious thoughts and feelings, guide them through life":

Therapist: Imagine yourself as the driver of a bus called "My Life." Along your route, you pick up some unruly passengers, which are unwanted anxiety-related thoughts that your mind serves up for you. These passengers intimidate you as you drive along your chosen route. Perhaps you can think of a recent [time] where you experienced anxiety. What are some of those statements that seem to be very intense and steer you off course? *[After writing each statement on a separate index card....the therapist reads the statement on the card...]* ...

Client: I feel I just had to respond. These thoughts seem to be so forceful and have such power over me...

Therapist: I will read the same passenger statements to you one more time. However, this time, why don't you just listen to the statements—they're just thoughts anyway. ...You can make a choice to be willing to have the thoughts *and* stay on the valued route no matter what the passengers say to you. Are you willing to do that?

Client: Okay. It will be hard, but I'll do it. (Eifert & Forsyth, 2005, pp. 197–199).

A final metaphorical strategy, which is another core ACT intervention with anxious clients, is the *tug-of-war* exercise. As clients become more mindfully aware of and emotionally honest about the totality of their internal experiences, they can begin to let go of the fight with anxious thoughts and feelings, what the ACT practitioner would refer to as the "anxiety monster." It is, after all, a fight that the individual is having with himself or herself, and therefore it is an exercise in futility that is destined to fail. Moreover, for the person of faith, it keeps him or her from living into the abundance or fullness of life promised by Jesus. As with the previous two metaphors, "dropping the rope" is another effective metaphorical exercise that helps clients understand that "the ability to recognize that a cherished strategy is destined to fail is really an acceptance move" (Hayes *et al.*, 2012, p. 276). Roemer and Orsillo point out that "we find the tug-of-war metaphor from ACT can be helpful to illustrate the way that the struggle actually keeps distress present." For example,

name the monster → make it something outside the self

> We ask clients to imagine their distress (sadness, anxiety, anger, pain, etc.) is a monster and that they are engaged in a tug-of-war with it, with a large pit between them. The distress monster is trying to pull them toward the pit, which is a deep abyss that they do not want to fall into, so they pull with all their might, using both hands and planting their feet. The harder they pull, the harder the monster pulls back. It seems like the only thing they can do to avoid falling into the pit is keep pulling. Yet there is another option—they could drop the rope. The monster would still be there, but they would no longer be moving toward the pit, and they would be able to do other things with their hands and feet rather than struggling with the monster. Mindfulness practice can be one example of "dropping the rope." We find that clients often take to this metaphor and actually imagine themselves dropping a rope as they make a choice *not* to struggle with their pain either during their formal practice or, most important, as they live their lives. As clients begin to practice "dropping the rope" or allowing their emotional experience and find that their internal experiences may not dissipate but do not intensify in the same ways, it often becomes easier for them to continue to practice (2009, p. 134).

It often becomes easier because, as we have learned from neuroscience, the regular practice of mindfulness meditation and contemplative prayer fundamentally alters brain circuitry in a way that prefrontal fibers and linkages are strengthened while limbic structures are soothed and calmed. Mindfully practicing "dropping the rope" when anxious thoughts and feelings come to mind, as they surely will in keeping with the brain's negativity bias and predisposition toward vigilant awareness, will intentionally fire and wire together prefrontal neurons in a way that keeps us "anchored" in the present moment of lived experience. Learning not to fight with the "anxiety monster" or the "anxious passengers on the bus," i.e., learning not to fight with ourselves, is of fundamental importance to our personal growth and healing as well as to the growth and healing of those in our care. Below is an excerpt of a counseling session that illustrates the use of the tug-of-war metaphor:

Therapist: So your mind, hands, and feet are all tied up in the struggle with anxiety?
Client: Yes, they pretty much are, and that is even more frightening than the anxiety itself...
Therapist: You could indeed spend all your energy fighting anxiety monsters until the end. But there is a different way, which is perhaps hard to think of while you're so busy fighting: *You*

could simply drop the rope! The hardest thing to see is that your job here is not to win the tug-of-war. Your job is to drop the rope…
Client: The fight is over and my hands are free. …
Therapist: But that won't stop [the anxiety monsters] from getting up and shouting at you, "Hey, pick up the rope. What's wrong with you?" What do you do then?
Client: I guess I have to listen, and I could pick up the rope—but I don't have to pick it up, right? (Eifert & Forsyth, 2005, pp. 150–151).

Mindfulness- and acceptance-based therapeutic approaches offer pastoral and spiritual caregivers and clinical practitioners an important framework for intervening effectively with anxious clients and congregants. The meditational practices, relaxation techniques, and metaphorical strategies associated with the various therapeutic modalities, e.g., MBCT and ACT, reflect an informed understanding of how we can best use the mind to calm an anxious brain when we are engaged in daily contemplative-meditational practice *and,* perhaps even more importantly, when we are not. Accumulating data from the ongoing brain-imaging studies of Sara W. Lazar, for example, "lend considerable neural evidence to the claims of meditators that practice improves their mood, their emotional regulation, and, in particular, their ability to handle stressful situations when not meditating" (2013, p. 291). The empirical studies continue to reveal, unambiguously, that as we engage in *regular* if not daily contemplative-meditational practices, that *over time* we can change the anatomical structures of the brain that in turn will produce an alteration in neural activity and functioning. This, to be sure, is the promise of neuroplasticity, the hope that we and those in our care can learn to center ourselves more fully in the totality of the present moment of our lived experience and be less anxious about tomorrow and the future. Contemplative practice, therefore, is not a temporary escape from "real life," nor is it a superficial panacea for the difficulties of life. Rather, as we use the mind to rewire the brain in our daily spiritual practice, we find that we are more relationally engaged with the fullness of our own lives and the lives of others, that calming the anxious brain is becoming a way of life.

Conclusion

For decades, we have watched *Star Trek* on television and at the movies, and in either case the show and/or film opens with the same familiar line: "Space: the final frontier." And to some extent this is true; it has only been in recent years that we have come to learn that the observable nighttime sky does not even begin to capture the fullness of the universe. In fact, what we are looking at on a clear night are *only* the contents of our own celestial neighborhood, namely, the Milky Way galaxy. Moreover, astronomy researchers are helping us to understand that even then we only see a tiny fraction of its contents, for within the Milky Way are hundreds of billions of stars. And beyond the Milky Way are perhaps an equal number of galaxies, give or take, each with a similar number of stars and in some cases more. Our own corner of the universe, to be sure, is rather average in comparison to other galactic regions that may each contain a trillion or more stars. Space, as the opening line boldly declares, is indeed a frontier of immense and staggering proportion, but it is not the only frontier let alone the final frontier. For example, oceanographers continue to amaze us with their discoveries of the deep blue seas, pointing out that despite all the data collected in recent years we have only explored a tiny percentage of the earth's oceans. The oceans on this planet therefore represent an additional frontier in terms of exploration and discovery. And, as we have been learning throughout this study, there is yet another frontier of scientific research, which in its own way is equally and even more extraordinary than the other frontiers. We can only imagine what we will discover come the conclusion of the "Brain Activity Map Project," when the human brain is finally "mapped" in greater detail similar to the human genome project. Already we have some awareness of the brain's immensely complex nature, a sort of "universe" in our own head that parallels in certain ways the universe surrounding us in outer space. Even now, before the brain is mapped more extensively, we know that it contains more than a hundred billion neurons, and that each neuron is connected to other neurons through ten thousand or more synaptic linkages. If we attempt the math, we find that there are hundreds of trillions of synaptic connections linking the brain's neural groupings, or as Siegel calculated ten to the millionth power or ten times ten one million times. The vast number of synapses connecting the neurons in the brain is believed to exceed the number of atoms in the universe, so that even if we wanted to we would not live long enough to count them all or even begin to experience them all in a single lifetime.

In mapping the brain more extensively in the coming years, it is hoped by some that a more precise understanding of mental illness and psychological distress will begin to emerge. Heretofore psychiatrists, psychotherapists, pastoral counselors, and by extension pastoral and spiritual caregivers have had to rely on the *Diagnostic and Statistical Manual of Mental Disorders* (*DSM*) for assessing mental illnesses and psychological disorders, all the while knowing that it is an imprecise assessment tool to say the least. Even with the publication of the fifth edition (*DSM-V*), we are no closer to understanding the neural basis of psychological conditions and disorders. The National Institutes of Mental Health (NIMH), for example, and in particular its director, Dr. Thomas Insel, has "criticized the new manual for defining mental disorders based on symptoms rather than underlying biological causes" (Friedman, 2013, p. D3). What the NIMH is therefore seeking is a neurological approach to the treatment of mental and psychological disorders, one that with more scientific precision can locate a particular disorder within specific regions of the brain. As the science of neuroimaging continues to evolve, we will find "new ways of classifying mental disorders based on neurobiological measures and dimensions of behavior, like a tendency toward anxiety or disorganized thinking" (Friedman, 2013, p. D3). One can only imagine how beneficial this will be, not only scientifically but also therapeutically, as clients and congregants feel less shame for perceiving that they are somehow the cause of their own psychological distress. In the coming years, mental and psychological conditions will be diagnosed more precisely as brain disorders, as neuroimaging helps us identify the specific biomarkers in the brain. We will, in other words, rely less on *DSM* symptomatology for assessing and treating these disorders, which so often at the present time leaves the practitioner having to make a sort of impressionistic diagnosis with less than precise empirical criteria. Richard Friedman, the renowned professor of clinical psychiatry at Weill Cornell Medical College, points out that there was really little need for a new edition of the *DSM*: "There is little groundbreaking science that would redefine our diagnostic categories, and some of the changes appear to risk pathologizing everyday human misery" (2013, D3). As we continue to understand more of the neurobiology of mental and psychological disorders, we can help those in our care reframe and normalize their particular "disorder" as something more reflective of human development and experience and less a matter of personal weakness and failure.

This will also shed more light on the "neuroplastic principle," and deepen our understanding of the nature of self-directed neuroplasticity. The coming years hold great promise for the continued exploration of this new "frontier," the internal "universe" of mind and brain. As we have already discovered in chapter one, the human brain, far from being fixed, static, and unchanging after a certain age or following the formative years of life, has a profound capacity for changing and transforming its own functioning *and* structure throughout the lifespan. Thus, the potential for neuroplasticity that is abundantly obvious in the early years of life extends across the entire human life cycle, from the beginning until the very end of life. Pastoral and spiritual practitioners can begin incorporating this revolutionary discovery into their work, specifically educating clients and congregants about the connection between the neuroplastic principle and the cultivation of a daily contemplative-meditational practice. At the same time, we will also want to keep in mind the flip side of the equation, the equally important finding that while the brain is indeed built for change, it is hardwired at the moment to privilege negativity over positivity as well as anxious awareness over mindful awareness. The limbic structures of the brain, including the amygdala and the hippocampus, run far deeper than the higher-order executive structures of the prefrontal cortex, which is a more recent neural development and as such is not at this point of time as thoroughly integrated into the brain. For those of us who practice pastoral and spiritual care as well as pastoral counseling and psychotherapy, it is very important that we do our work in a way that helps the client or congregant build up more cortical structure while learning to calm the anxious activity of the limbic system. As we discussed in chapter three, this presupposes that we are taking great care not to introduce, directly and/or indirectly, any theological or psychological construct, e.g., an unexamined theology of original sin, that may even inadvertently prompt an anxious client or congregant to worry more and not less about the present and future. The promise of neuroplasticity is that we can calm the fear and stress regions of the brain, quintessentially through a daily practice of mindfulness meditation and contemplative prayer. This assumes a paradigm shift that elevates contemplative spiritual practice to a place of comparable importance with religious belief and doctrine, for as we noted in chapter four the health benefits of a daily contemplative-meditational practice, spiritual and psychophysiological, are potentially quite significant. Finally, in chapter five, we introduced several therapeutic modalities that intentionally incorporate the findings of neuroscience into clinical practice. Mindfulness- and acceptance-based approaches, in particular MBCT and ACT, offer us a more precise therapeutic framework for our work with anxious clients and congregants.

Additionally, in chapter six, I presented specific case material and vignettes that illustrate the practical benefits of mindfulness and acceptance techniques and practices. Through the regular use of mindfulness meditations, reflective exercises, and contemplative practices, we see that it is possible over time to use the mind to rewire the brain.

My hope is that pastoral and spiritual caregivers, pastoral counselors, and even psychotherapists will find this a helpful resource for framing their work in an age of neuroscience, that perhaps even a mindfulness-based pastoral and spiritual care and a mindfulness-based pastoral counseling can emerge in the coming years. In much the same way that Siegel articulates his vision for the "mindful therapist" and for the development of a mindfulness-based psychotherapy, I, too, would encourage those of us in the fields of pastoral and spiritual care and pastoral counseling to formulate a similar vision for the mindful pastoral caregiver, the mindful pastoral counselor, the mindful spiritual director, and so on. This will take the findings I have presented in this study even further, continuing to help those in our care to rewire the mind and brain on a daily basis. In so doing, we will more effectively support the growth and healing of clients and congregants, helping them to be less anxious about tomorrow, to be more centered in the gift of the present moment, ultimately to live into the peace and joy of abundant life.

References

Altman, D. (2010). *The mindfulness code: Keys for overcoming stress, anxiety, fear, and unhappiness*. Novato, CA: New World Library.

American Psychiatric Association. (2013). *Diagnostic and statistical manual of mental disorders: DSM-V-TR*. Washington, D.C.: Author.

Barbour, I. (1997). *Religion and science: Historical and contemporary issues*. San Francisco: Harper.

Barrett, J. (2011). *Cognitive science, religion, and theology: From human minds to divine minds*. West Conshohocken, PA: Templeton.

Beauregard, M. (2007). *The spiritual brain: A neuroscientist's case for the existence of the soul*. New York: Harper.

Benson, H. (1975). *The relaxation response*. New York: William Morrow.

Bernstein, R. (1995, April 5). Who saved civilization? The Irish, that's who! [Review of the book, *How the Irish saved civilization*, by Thomas Cahill]. *The New York Times Book Review*.

Bingaman, K. (2011). The art of contemplative and mindfulness practice: Incorporating the findings of neuroscience into pastoral counseling. *Pastoral Psychology, 60*(3), 477-489.

Bingaman, K. (2012). Beyond original sin: A paradigm shift for the neuroscience. *Pastoral Psychology, 61*(4), 411-422.

Bingaman, K. (2013). The promise of neuroplasticity for pastoral care and counseling. *Pastoral Psychology, 62*(5), 549-560.

Bobrow, J. (2003). Moments of truth – truths of moment. In J. Safran (Ed.), *Psychoanalysis and Buddhism: An unfolding dialogue* (pp. 199-249). Boston: Wisdom Publications.

Brach, T. (2003). *Radical acceptance: Embracing your life with the heart of a Buddha*. New York: Bantam.

Brach, T. (2012). *True refuge: Finding peace and freedom in your own awakened heart*. New York: Bantam.

Bulkeley, K. (2005a). Religion and brain-mind science: Dreaming the future. In K. Bulkeley (Ed.), *Soul, psyche, and brain: New directions in the study of religion and brain-mind science* (pp. 219-241). New York: Palgrave Macmillan.

Bulkeley, K. (2005b). *The wondering brain: Thinking about religion with and beyond cognitive neuroscience*. New York: Routledge.

Calvin, J. (1960). *Institutes of the Christian religion*. J.T. McNeill (Ed.). Louisville: Westminster John Knox.

Capps, D. (1993). *The depleted self: Sin in a narcissistic age*. Minneapolis: Fortress.

Chopp, R. (1997). Theorizing feminist theology. In R. Chopp & S.G. Davaney (Eds.), *Horizons in feminist theology: Identity, tradition, and norms* (pp. 215–231). Minneapolis: Augsburg Fortress.

Coffman, S. *et al.* (2006). Mindfulness-based cognitive therapy for prevention of depressive relapse. In R.A. Baer (Ed.), *Mindfulness-based treatment approaches* (pp. 31–50). New York: Academic Press.

Davidson, R.J. (2012). *The emotional life of your brain: How its unique patterns affect the way you think, feel, and live—and how you can change them.* New York: Plume.

Eifert, G., & Forsyth, J. (2005). *Acceptance and commitment therapy for anxiety disorders: A practitioner's treatment guide to using mindfulness, acceptance, and values-based behavior change strategies.* Oakland, CA: New Harbinger.

Ellis, A. (2003). *Anger: How to live with and without it.* New York: Citadel.

Fredrickson, B. (2009). *Positivity: Top-notch research reveals the 3 to 1 ratio that will change your life.* New York: Three Rivers.

Freud, S. (1964/1940). An outline of psycho-analysis. In J. Strachey (Ed. and Trans.), *The standard edition of the complete psychological works of Sigmund Freud* (Vol. 23, pp. 144–207). London: Hogarth.

Friedman, R. (2013, May 20). The book stops here. *The New York Times*, p. D3.

Gazzaniga, M. (2005). *The ethical brain.* New York: Dana Press.

Gazzaniga, M. (2008). *Human: The science behind what makes us unique.* New York: Ecco/HarperCollins.

Gottman, J. (1995). *Why marriages succeed or fail: And how you can make yours last.* New York: Simon and Schuster.

Gottman, J. (1999). *The seven principles for making marriage work.* New York: Three Rivers.

Hanh, T.N. (2006). *The energy of prayer: How to deepen your spiritual practice.* Berkeley: Parallax.

Hanh, T.N. (2007). *Living Buddha, living Christ.* New York: Riverhead.

Hanson, R. (2009). *Buddha's brain: The practical neuroscience of happiness, love, and wisdom.* Oakland: New Harbinger.

Hayes, S. *et al.* (2012). *Acceptance and commitment therapy: The process and practice of mindful change.* New York: Guilford.

Herlihy, D. (1997). *The black death and the transformation of the West.* Cambridge, MA: Harvard.

Hogue, D. (2003). *Remembering the future, imagining the past: Story, ritual, and the human brain.* Cleveland: Pilgrim.

Ignatius of Loyola. (1991). *Ignatius of Loyola: Spiritual exercises and selected works (Classics of western spirituality).* G.E. Ganss, S.J. (Ed.). New York: Paulist.

Jones, A. (2006). *Common prayer on common ground: A vision of Anglican orthodoxy.* New York: Morehouse.

Kabat-Zinn, J. (2011). Some clinical applications of mindfulness meditation in medicine and psychiatry: The case of mindfulness-based stress reduction (MBSR). In J. Kabat-Zinn & R. Davidson (Eds.), *The mind's own physician: A scientific dialogue with the Dalai Lama on the healing power of meditation* (pp. 35–47). Oakland, CA: New Harbinger.

Kabat-Zinn, J. & Davidson, R. (2011a). A confluence of streams and a flowering of possibilities. In J. Kabat-Zinn & R. Davidson (Eds.), *The mind's own physician: A scientific dialogue with the Dalai Lama on the healing power of meditation* (pp. 1–19). Oakland, CA: New Harbinger.

Kabat-Zinn, J. & Davidson, R. (2011b). Advances in basic and clinical research on meditation in the five years following Mind and Life XIII: 2006–2011. In J. Kabat-Zinn & R. Davidson (Eds.), *The mind's own physician: A scientific dialogue with the Dalai Lama on the healing power of meditation* (pp. 207–221). Oakland, CA: New Harbinger.

Kandel, E. (2006). *In search of memory: The emergence of a new science of mind.* New York: W.W. Norton.

Kandel, E. *et al.* (2013). *Principles of neural science.* New York: McGraw-Hill.

Keating, T. (1994). *Intimacy with God: An introduction to Centering Prayer.* New York: Crossroad.

Keating, T. (2006). *Open heart, open mind: The contemplative dimension of the gospel*. New York: Continuum.

Kockelmans, J. (1994). *Edmund Husserl's phenomenology*. West Lafayette, IN: Purdue University.

Lazar, S.W. (2013). The neurobiology of mindfulness. In C. Germer, R. Siegel, & P. Fulton (Eds.), *Mindfulness and psychotherapy* (pp. 282-291). New York: Guilford.

LeDoux, J. (2002). *Synaptic self: How our brains become who we are*. New York: Viking.

Markoff, J. (2013, February 18). Obama seeking to boost study of the human brain. *The New York Times*, p. A1.

Martin S.J., J. (2010). *The Jesuit guide to (almost) everything: A spirituality for real life*. New York: Harper.

May, G. (1991). *Addiction and grace: Love and spirituality in the healing of addictions*. San Francisco: Harper.

McEwen, B. (2002). *The end of stress as we know it*. Washington, D.C.: John Henry.

Merton, T. (1960). *Spiritual direction and meditation*. Collegeville, MN: Liturgical Press.

Merton, T. (1971). *Contemplative prayer*. New York: Image Books.

Merton, T. (2007). *New seeds of contemplation*. New York: New Directions.

Newberg, A., D'Aquili, E., & Rause, V. (2002). *Why God won't go away: Brain science and the biology of belief*. New York: Ballantine.

Newberg, A. (2009). *How God changes your brain: Breakthrough findings from a leading neuroscientist*. New York: Ballantine.

Newberg, A. (2010). *Principles of neurotheology*. Farnham, Surrey UK: Ashgate.

Orsillo, S. & Roemer, L. (2011). *The mindful way through anxiety: Break free from chronic worry and reclaim your life*. New York: Guilford.

Osteen, J. (2010). *Become a better you: Seven keys to improving your life every day*. Philadelphia: Running Press.

Pagels, E. (1989). *Adam, Eve, and the serpent*. New York: Vintage.

Pennington, M.B. (2008). *Centering Prayer: Renewing an ancient Christian prayer form*. New York: Image Books.

Porges, S. (2011). *The polyvagal theory: Neurophysiological foundations of emotions, attachment, communication, and self-regulation*. New York: W.W. Norton.

Ramachandran, V.S. (2011). *The tell-tale brain: A neuroscientist's quest for what makes us human*. New York: W.W. Norton.

Ricard, M. (2011). Meditation-based clinical interventions: Science, practice, and implementation. In J. Kabat-Zinn & R. Davidson (Eds.), *The mind's own physician: A scientific dialogue with the Dalai Lama on the healing power of meditation* (pp. 21–26). Oakland, CA: New Harbinger.

Ricoeur, P. (2004). *The conflict of interpretations: Essays in hermeneutics*. D. Ihde (Ed.). London: Continuum.

Roemer, L. *et al.* (2006). Incorporating mindfulness- and acceptance-based strategies in the treatment of generalized anxiety disorder. In R.A. Baer (Ed.), *Mindfulness-based treatment approaches* (pp. 51–74). New York: Academic Press.

Roemer, L. & Orsillo, S. (2009). *Mindfulness- and acceptance-based behavioral therapies in practice*. New York: Guilford.

Rosenfeld, D. (Executive Producer), & Malick, T. (Director). (2011). *The tree of life* [Motion Picture]. United States: River Road Entertainment.

Schwartz, J.M. (2003). *The mind and the brain: Neuroplasticity and the power of mental force*. New York: Regan Books.

Segal, Z. (2011). Mindfulness-based cognitive therapy and the prevention of relapse in recurrent depression. In J. Kabat-Zinn & R. Davidson (Eds.), *The mind's own physician: A scientific dialogue with the Dalai Lama on the healing power of meditation* (pp. 102–110). Oakland, CA: New Harbinger.

Segal, Z. *et. al.* (2013). *Mindfulness-based cognitive therapy for depression*. New York: Guilford.

Seligman, M. (1990). *Learned optimism: How to change your mind and your life*. New York: Vintage.

Shakespeare, W. (1978). *Hamlet.* A.L. Rowse (Ed.). New York: Longmeadow Press.

Siegel, D. (2007). *The mindful brain: Reflection and attunement in the cultivation of well-being.* New York: W.W. Norton.

Siegel, D. (2010). *The mindful therapist: A clinician's guide to mindsight and neural integration.* New York: W.W. Norton.

Siegel, D. (2011). *Mindsight: The new science of personal transformation.* New York: Bantam.

Singer, W. (2011). Some reflections on the evolution and nature of mind and self, and their implications for humanity. In J. Kabat-Zinn & R. Davidson (Eds.), *The mind's own physician: A scientific dialogue with the Dalai Lama on the healing power of meditation* (pp. 185–192). Oakland, CA: New Harbinger.

Smith, A. & Riedel-Pfaefflin, U. (2004). *Siblings by choice: Race, gender, & violence.* Atlanta, GA: Chalice.

Snyderman, R. (2011). Meditation and the future of health care. In J. Kabat-Zinn & R. Davidson (Eds.), *The mind's own physician: A scientific dialogue with the Dalai Lama on the healing power of meditation* (pp. 179–185). Oakland, CA: New Harbinger.

Taylor, J. Bolte (2009). *My stroke of insight: A brain scientist's personal journey.* New York: Viking.

Tillich, P. (1975). *Systematic theology: Vol. 2. Existence and the Christ.* Chicago: University of Chicago.

Tillich, P. (1999). Aspects of a religious analysis of culture. In F.F. Church (Ed.), *The essential Tillich: An anthology of the writings of Paul Tillich* (pp. 101–111). Chicago: University of Chicago.

Tolle, E. (2005). *A new earth: Awakening to your life's purpose.* New York: Penguin.

Tracy, D. (1994). *Plurality and ambiguity: Hermeneutics, religion, hope.* Chicago: University of Chicago.

Index

About the Author

Kirk A. Bingaman, Ph.D. is Associate Professor of Pastoral Care & Counseling at Fordham University. He is a Licensed Mental Health Counselor (LMHC) in New York and a Fellow with the American Association of Pastoral Counselors (AAPC). His previous books include *Freud and Faith: Living in the Tension* (SUNY) and *Treating the New Anxiety: A Cognitive-Theological Approach* (Jason Aronson).